DAN CODY'S YACHT

BY ANTHONY GIARDINA

★

★

DRAMATISTS
PLAY SERVICE
INC.

2

CHARACTERS

KEVIN O'NEILL

CARA RUSSO

CATHY CONZ

ANGELA RUSSO

CONOR O'NEILL

GEOFF HOSMER

PAMELA HOSMER

ALICE TUAN

SETTING

The play takes place in various locations in and around the fictional towns of Stillwell and Patchett, Massachusetts—both towns in the far outer ring of suburbs around Boston—from September 2014 to June of 2016.

NOTE

In several speeches, long and short, I've used parenthetical indentations to break up the speech. The intention is not to suggest that the characters speak in paragraphs, but that something has happened within the speech to require a shifting, either up and down, that should happen more quickly than would be indicated by the use of a beat.

Also, I've used the / and \ notations to indicate when characters are stepping over each other's dialogue.

The poem "Trees" was written by Grace Howe. Permission to use the poem in performance has been granted by the poet, for no additional royalty fee.

DAN CODY'S YACHT

ACT ONE

Scene 1

A high school classroom. Two chairs, a school desk.

Cara Russo, late 30s, attractive, dressed in teacher garb but with some attention to style. Tired, though. It's the end of a long day of teaching.

Kevin O'Neill, mid-40s, in a very good suit. A handsome guy, confident and ready to be amused.

An after-school conference. Cara and Kevin, both seated in chairs.

KEVIN. So you gave him an F because it was clear he hadn't read the book.

CARA. *(Moves hair out of her eyes.)* That's basically it, yes.

> *Beat. He regards her.*

KEVIN. And the book was *The Great Gatsby*?

> *Is she intimidated by him, or by his manner, or by something in the question itself? Whatever, she fights it.*

CARA. Correct.

KEVIN. He gets no credit for trying to fake his way through?

> *She smiles politely.*

Can I see the paper?

> *She hands it to him. He takes out a pair of glasses, proceeds to read. Then he looks up at the lighting.*

Jesus. How are these kids supposed to—

He looks at her.

You'll go blind at fifty. You have a good pension? Teachers—? I should know this.

CARA. I have an excellent pension.

KEVIN. Good, then.

He continues to look at her, smiling, until she becomes uncomfortable.

CARA. You were going to read the paper.

KEVIN. Right.

He reads, amused.

Well, he does say some good things. "Money corrupts." Now there's something I haven't heard before.

CARA. Unfortunately what he's saying has nothing to do with the book.

KEVIN. So an F. *(Bristles dramatically.)* Harsh.

She holds her ground, and he continues to stare at her, as if trying to figure something out.

How are you teaching it?

CARA. Excuse me?

KEVIN. How are you—what approach are you taking? Do you have a—is there a point of view you're trying to put over?

CARA. Mr. O'Neill.

KEVIN. Kevin.

CARA. Everyone intelligent who reads a book—every *teacher*—has a point of view.

KEVIN. *(A smile.)* Are you teaching them to hate money?

Beat. In reply, she simply looks at him.

Because what an opportunity. Yes? In this select high school with terrible lighting.

He takes a card out of his pocket and writes something on the back of it.

And you live in Patchett, don't you? That depressed little mill town—*ex*-mill town across the river. You drive over that river every morning and come to this Brigadoon, to confront a sea of bland,

8

handsome, one might even say gorgeous young faces—sixteen, eighteen, unmarked. Lacrosse. Mount Desert Island. If they've ever worked they've worked as *lifeguards*. *Camp* counselors.

CARA. *(Still trying to be polite, smiling, though challenged.)* If this is an accusation, if you're suggesting I'm bringing / a bias—

KEVIN. These kids \ who can fake reading a book, get an F on a term paper, and still most likely have their paths greased to, at the very least, *Wesleyan*. What an opportunity. This book. To teach them—well, you tell me.

> All of this has been said with great charm. They look at each other.

CARA. The operative words, I would think—

KEVIN. Yes?

CARA. In what you've just said. Are "most likely."

> Beat. She's gotten his attention.

"Most likely" have their paths greased to, at the very least, Wesleyan. "Most likely" but not "most certainly."

> She's touched something. He doesn't let her know. Tries not to let her know. But she knows.

You and I both know, Mr. O'Neill—

KEVIN. Kevin.

CARA. Excuse me. I'm actually not comfortable with Kevin.

> As she continues to speak, Kevin reaches deftly into his pocket, removes his billfold and counts out a number of bills, folds them, and slides them across the adjoining desk toward her.

—That simple attendance at this school is no guarantee of getting in anywhere at all.

> At some point during this last speech, she has become fixated on the cash that's been laid before her.

Excuse me.

> He smiles.

Do I need to call the—

KEVIN. What? The school custodian? The principal's office? Have I just assaulted you, Ms. Russo?

9

CARA. *(Hard-nosed.)* Put them back please.

KEVIN. Let's—shall we?—let's give it ten seconds.

CARA. Put them away.

KEVIN. Ten seconds.

> *She stares him down for only three or four seconds, before she stands, goes for her pocketbook, a clear gesture that this is over.*

Okay, let's call that ten seconds. I just want you to know the amount I've just placed in front of you is only sufficient to raise the grade from an F to a D. I wouldn't insult you by / pretending—

CARA. You're my \ last conference, Mr. O'Neill.

> *She's deeply embarrassed now. Can't look at him.*
>
> *He looks at his watch. Stands as well.*

KEVIN. Yes. Back to the office.

> *But he doesn't go.*

Incorruptible Cara Russo. I've heard about it, now I've seen it for myself. Chosen by her peers to be the powerful voice of the teachers in our town's current, ill-advised plunge into liberal American mediocrity. The proposal to meld the two school districts—depressed Patchett, thriving Stillwell. To join the drug-addicted, poverty-ridden, low-achieving children of your little town to the drug-addicted but still high-achieving children of mine.

CARA. I'll be going now, Mr. O'Neill. If you wouldn't mind—

> *She hoists her pocketbook over her shoulder, gestures that he should leave.*
>
> *But he doesn't leave.*

KEVIN. Don't do it.

CARA. Don't do what?

KEVIN. Don't use your considerable power on behalf of an old, overworked, melting-pot idea. We don't *melt* here, Cara Russo. Not anymore. Look, why don't we have a seat.

CARA. Mr. O'Neill, I'm a single parent. It's four o'clock. I'd like to get home, have a run, make sure my daughter has something to eat, then prepare for what will no doubt be a very long meeting on this very issue. Having ended the day by having to refuse a bribe, I'd say the challenges of the week have just come to a head.

KEVIN. What are you making?

    Beat.

For dinner. I could use some ideas. I'm a single parent myself. I'm bringing up Conor alone.

    He takes a seat, draws it far away from her, to assure her of her safety.

And don't think please that this is a come-on. I'm gay. Came out ten years ago. Should have done it sooner, but I was *enjoying* a double life so much. Shame on me.

    Beat.

I bought truffle oil. I was in Whole Foods, I said, I bet that's good. Now it sits on the shelf.

CARA. *(Intrigued by him in spite of herself, though still not giving an inch.)* What—what is it you do, Mr. O'Neill? I'm curious what a man like you does.

KEVIN. *(Fully taking in her imputation.)* "A man like me." I'm in private equity.

CARA. Ah. Is that—are you—is that hedge funds?

KEVIN. I've never known what people mean by that phrase, but if that's useful to you, all right. It's not accurate, but all right. And now, please, there's something I want to propose to you.

CARA. Something that involves / money—

KEVIN. You live \ in a house in Patchett that could use some repairs.

CARA. How is it you know my house?

KEVIN. I've driven past it. Relax, this is not stalking we're talking about, I *prepare* myself for meetings, Ms. Russo.

CARA. Something you learn to do, I suppose, in private equity. Check out the houses of / potential—

KEVIN. You have a \ daughter who attends the high school over there. Bright girl, I'm sure. But Patchett High School does not produce *killers.* Or very much else, as far as I can see. The fact is, there is no "academic excellence" in Patchett, and you know it. Shall I go on?

CARA. Only because I can't imagine where this is headed.

KEVIN. Incorruptible Cara Russo has been handed the golden opportunity to recommend that the two school districts merge. If this goes through, your bright, promising daughter will be deposited in a high-achieving, award-winning high school whose students, those who wind up below the Ivies, those are the ones who are considered disappointments. So this would solve your problem neatly, wouldn't it?

> He leans forward in his seat. A kind of sales pitch, but sincere and convincing.

Because in your heart of hearts you fear for your daughter in this climate. You fear for her future at a state school, followed by a nursing career. And crippling debt. Oh, America, land that I love.

CARA. Mr. O'Neill, I can absolutely assure you that my vote on this committee is not going to be compromised in any way by my having a daughter who stands to / benefit.

KEVIN. Wonderful. \ But this is going to come down to a town vote, isn't it? And even if the vote goes against you, I'm guessing you'd still like to get your daughter into this school.

CARA. Where is this heading? Please. My very limited free time is running out.

KEVIN. On Thursday nights, once a month, in my house on Belstrom Road in Stillwell, I host a very informal investment party. A small group of locals. We pool our money. We make investments which we call "fun." I'm not sure what "fun" means when it comes to money, but then I'm not sure what a hedge fund is. Nonetheless, I'm tendering an invitation.

> A long pause. She looks at him, staggered by the absurdity of the invitation but also amused at how far he's willing to go.

CARA. Do you really live in a world where you believe everyone has money to play with?

KEVIN. Most people do. They just don't know it.

CARA. But you, with your great financial acumen, are able to pluck opportunity out of thin air.

KEVIN. Look at you. You have a house. What do you do with it? I assume you have some equity, but you'd never think of playing with it in some serious way.

CARA. Some of us consider our money a little too precious to play with, Mr. O'Neill. So thank you very much, but now it's time for you to let me go run.

KEVIN. I'm not keeping you here. Actually.

> *Beat.*

You could have left at any point over the last ten minutes. You're finding me obnoxious, which I am, but somewhere in that very good head of yours, you do suspect the truth. Which is that you've just gotten lucky.

CARA. Oh have I?

KEVIN. It's maddening to me how people like you live. Forgive me, I shouldn't say "maddening." I should say that it breaks my heart. Paying your mortgage dutifully, squirreling away little scraps of money for college, hoping against hope that the geniuses on Wall Street don't do something colossally stupid again to render all your self-restraint worthless. You're too smart to leave yourself open to that. Come to my house. Forget civic largesse and being careful. Make some *money*. I serve nice hors d'oeuvres from Whole Foods. Get serious. Fight like hell for your daughter.

CARA. Explain to me, please, how coming to your house and eating hors d'oeurves equals fighting like hell for my daughter?

KEVIN. You could make enough money to move here. I think you can still find something—a cottage—for six hundred thousand. Seems like a fortune, I know, but I'm very good. Whatever name you want to put on what I do, I'm very good at it. And I'm not trying to sell you anything false. Come to my house and see how it feels. That's all. Don't give me a penny to invest until you've checked me out thoroughly. *Talk* to my investors. It's a club. Good cheese, good wine, Miles Davis on the stereo. Yo-Yo Ma. Why are you smiling?

CARA. I'm just imagining the glories of combining Yo-Yo Ma and financial chicanery.

KEVIN. Is has to be chicanery, does it? This can't be genuine.

CARA. *(Beat.)* I think my own financial plans are quite sound, thank you.

KEVIN. Are they? Are they really? Do you really believe that? Did you sleep through 2008? It was only six years ago—have you forgotten it already?

He's opened a weakness in her which she tries to cover.

I drove by your house. I was moved. That's all, really. I was moved by the—roof. It's a sad roof. Sometimes I drive through parts of the state just to look. I don't want to live an enclosed life.

This has seemed, strangely, like a genuine moment.

CARA. Perhaps—if you want to break out of your enclosure—you shouldn't begin by trying to bribe your son's teacher.

He reaches into his billfold, takes out the money he offered her, places it on the desk.

KEVIN. Take a look.

CARA. I don't need to count.

KEVIN. Take a look. A close look.

Finally she does. He holds it up for her. It's play money. He smiles.

Not quite Monopoly money, but close. You see, I was only testing you. And by the way, you passed.

CARA. I don't like to be played with.

KEVIN. I'm sorry. Sometimes I can't help myself. I know, I go too far. I apologize / for this.

CARA. Thank you \ very much for your offer. I'm due back to my sad roof now.

KEVIN. Don't tell me you'll come. Just—think about it.

He takes out a card, writes his address on the back.

Here's my address. Thursday nights. Every third Thursday of the month. Which would make our next meeting in two weeks. Seven o'clock. We start off with a drink. We spend an hour or so talking about the market. Then we get down to it.

He continues to hold out his card, insistent. When she doesn't take it, he puts it down in front of her.

Beat.

Could I have the paper?

Cara hands him his son's paper.

I'll go over this with Conor. Give him the F. Let this be what they call a "learning experience." The thing is, I actually love this book. Maybe I haven't made that clear. And I'm not—I've never been—a sophisticated reader. But what I love is the part of Gatsby that really is uncorruptible. It's a quality I admire.

CARA. *(Beat.)* Good afternoon, Mr. O'Neill.

She moves past him.

KEVIN. There's a part of the novel—I'll tell Conor to take a look at it, but maybe you should, too. It's often overlooked. Remember Dan Cody's yacht? Young Gatsby on the shore, a lost boy, looking for something, anything, really, to save him from his closed, limited life. And this gaudy yacht pulls up. He knows enough not to question the gaudiness. He finds a rowboat and he rows like hell to get on board. Because he knows something. Opportunity has just arrived.

She continues to look at him a moment.

Lights down.

Scene 2

Cara's house. Cara has come home from a meeting. It's late. She's tired. It's early fall, a week or so after the time of the first scene, her meeting with Kevin. She wears a coat and is just taking it off when her friend Cathy comes in, in a rush.

Cathy is more rough-hewn working class in manner and voice than Cara.

CARA. Hey.

CATHY. Britney left her book here. Sorry. Can I barge in on Angela?

CARA. *(Calling off.)* Angela!

Angela comes on. A plain girl, not unpretty. Perhaps a bit overweight. No one's idea of a future "killer."

CATHY. Britney left her copy of *Exodus.*

Angela and Cara share a look, then Angela goes off to get

the book.

CARA. Cathy.

CATHY. What?

CARA. Buttons.

> *Cara redoes the buttons on Cathy's coat. There's a tenderness between these two.*

CATHY. I was in a hurry. How was the meeting?

> *Angela comes on, hands Cathy a well-used paperback copy of* Exodus, *then starts to go.*

CARA. Did you eat?

ANGELA. Of course.

> *She exits.*

CARA. *Exodus?* They're reading *Exodus?*

CATHY. High school can't afford to buy new books.

CARA. I should have known this. An English teacher—

CATHY. *(Finishing her sentence for her.)* —is busy. Can't ask every question.

CARA. Last semester they spent six weeks on *To Kill a Mockingbird.*

CATHY. We have a problem there?

CARA. Cathy, you can't go into a college interview with nothing more sophisticated to talk about than Atticus Finch. My class in Stillwell is reading *Beloved.*

CATHY. Well, that's good. That they're reading *Beloved.* And maybe the reason you don't know that over here on this side of the river they're reading *Exodus* is because you're busy at meetings making sure we can ship them over there so that they can *all* read *Beloved.* They can all be smart as a whip and wow the college admissions people. They won't know who the hell they are, but they'll all be smart.

> *Cara finds this frustrating; at the same time, she counts on Cathy for this sort of thing.*

CARA. Do you want a drink?

CATHY. Can't. Got to bring home *Exodus* for my girl.

CARA. *(Sits, takes her shoes off.)* Shut up.

CATHY. You shut up. This is probably the copy I read twenty years ago. At good old Patchett High. It was good. Made me cry. Britney made debate.

CARA. Congratulations.

Cara helps herself to a glass of wine.

CATHY. "Resolved." How does it work? They stand up. Argue. I don't quite understand.

CARA. You know, I really hate it when you try to pretend you're stupid.

CATHY. Never have made debate over there. Those kids? Never. Give her confidence to do that.

CARA. There's a man from Stillwell wants to make me a pile of money in exchange for my voting no on this committee.

CATHY. No. Who?

CARA. I can't tell you.

CATHY. Russian? A Jap?

They're both laughing.

CARA. Will you stop? What you're doing is worse. "We will lose our identity." Is our identity that plastic?

Beat. A fault line in their relationship. Cathy looks hesitantly thoughtful.

What?

CATHY. Nothing. "Plastic"?

CARA. You don't like that word? Give me a better one.

CATHY. All right—how about vulnerable, you like that one? Our high school is our town. We lose that, what have we got? We ship our kids over the river to become second-class citizens, they come back, how do they respect anything here? Vulnerable good enough for you?

CARA. I haven't decided what I'm going to recommend.

CATHY. You've decided. How can you decide any different from what you've decided. We've got an old pitiful school where the kids are reading copies of *Exodus* scotch-taped together. And we are lucky enough to have beside us Stuck-Up High.

17

CARA. Are we going out for a drink Friday night? Are we going out for a drink or have you decided you hate me because I just may vote to turn our kids into second-class citizens?

CATHY. I don't hate you. I just wish you wouldn't deflect everything I'm saying.

CARA. Are we going out for a drink?

CATHY. Of course we are.

CARA. Good. Nachos. A drink. It's been a week.

CATHY. How soon would it happen?

CARA. What?

CATHY. If we merged with them over there?

CARA. I don't know. *If* we recommend, *if* the two towns vote to affirm it, it could happen next year.

CATHY. So they'll be seniors.

CARA. Yes.

CATHY. Good year, senior year. If you're in a place where everybody knows you.

CARA. Stop. Please. I am one vote.

CATHY. Yeah, but you're an important one. They listen to you. I looked up the debate team over there. Smart kids. Slotnick. Liebowicz. Chan. Patel. How's my Britney going to compete with those kids?

CARA. Maybe she could.

CATHY. Okay.

CARA. Maybe she could. How will we know if we keep her here?

CATHY. Maybe we know, Cara. Maybe we're not that dumb.

Cara stands up, puts her hands on both sides of Cathy's head.

CARA. Okay. I listened. I hear you. I am going to do what's right. Try to, anyway. Don't bully me. Now go home. You're tired. And Britney needs her book.

CATHY. G'night.

Cathy starts to go.

CARA. Hey.

She calls Cathy back. They bump foreheads affectionately.

18

Nachos. Friday night.

> *Cathy exits.*

Angela.

> *Angela comes out, holding her own copy of* Exodus.

What did you eat?

ANGELA. You asked me that.

CARA. No, I asked did you eat. Not what.

ANGELA. Leftover mac and cheese.

CARA. How's *Exodus*?

> *She asks Angela to hand her the book.*

You didn't tell me. What, have you been hiding it under your bed?

ANGELA. No. I put it behind *Harry Potter*. You never look there.

> *Beat.*

I knew you'd be mad.

CARA. I'm going to have a talk with Mrs. Lenz. It's time we had a talk about the curriculum.

ANGELA. Fine.

CARA. She could choose something more challenging. She could ask parents for money and buy new books.

ANGELA. And some of them would actually give it.

> *Beat.*

CARA. How are you?

ANGELA. I'm okay.

CARA. Sorry I've been out so much.

ANGELA. It's okay.

CARA. How's Britney?

ANGELA. She made debate.

CARA. And you? Don't you want to go out for debate? Or for a play? What play are they doing this year?

ANGELA. *Godspell.* I don't sing.

CARA. *(Beat.)* You sing.

ANGELA. I have a test tomorrow.

Angela reaches out to receive the book. The cover comes off as Cara hands it to her. Cara is left holding the cover.

CARA. I know.

ANGELA. It's not a bad book.

CARA. No.

ANGELA. The cover's off, but it's not a bad book.

CARA. Yes.

ANGELA. Try to remember that.

Angela leaves.

Cara, left with the detached cover, looks at it, then looks around her house, taking it in. Suddenly frightened. She takes out the card Kevin handed her, looks at it, puts it away. She's frightened.

Sound of an indie-rock band* comes up, very loud. Cara's house disappears and Kevin's comes on. However minimal the set pieces, we should know immediately we've just gone radically upscale.

Scene 3

Kevin's house. Conor, Kevin's son, 16, gorgeous, standing over a plate of sushi, headphones on. Conor should have longish hair.

There should be a sense that the room has been decked out for a gathering. Sounds of a small group talking, socializing offstage.

Kevin comes on from the offstage kitchen area, followed by Geoff Hosmer. Kevin is carrying his laptop. He will immediately sit, open the laptop, and begin perusing it, even as he engages with Conor and Geoff at the opening of the scene.

Geoff is roughly Kevin's age, a family therapist with enormous inherited wealth. He's dressed casually, but any aficionado of

---

* In the New York production, the songs "My Girls" and "FloriDada" by Animal Collective were used as Conor's music, when it was heard. It is the responsibility of the licensee to clear the rights to any copyrighted music used in production. See note on songs/recordings at the back of this volume for more information.

clothing would be able to tell his clothes are very, very expensive. He's a model of relaxed suburban splendor. At the moment, he's carrying a wineglass in one hand and an open bottle of wine in the other.

Kevin and Geoff enter just as Conor has snuck a couple of handfuls of sushi. Sound down.

KEVIN. Hands off that stuff. That's for my guests.

Conor doesn't hear him.

CONOR. *(Taking off headphones.)* What?

GEOFF. Let him eat them. It's only Whole Foods sushi—your father is so cheap he will not spring for the real stuff. I'm going to call Minimora. They deliver.

KEVIN. Don't you dare. *(To Conor, as he sets himself up on a comfortable chair with his laptop.)* Anyway, time you went upstairs and hit the books. Books you won't read because you're—what? Too busy? *(To Geoff.)* Got an F on a paper.

GEOFF. No. What are you listening to?

CONOR. [Name of whatever band Conor is listening to.]*

GEOFF. No shit. I *love* [repeats the name of the band]. Let me have those.

He gestures that Conor should hand over the headphones.

KEVIN. Do not tell me that in your insanely overprivileged life you have time to listen to the garage bands he listens to.

GEOFF. My kids play it for me.

He puts on the headphones, begins to sing along with the song in falsetto. Kevin just stares at him in disgust.

CONOR. You guys are hilarious. Do you even like each other?

KEVIN. Hell no. He's the power structure in this town, so I've got to hang out with him.

---

* As there is something perfect about Animal Collective being Conor's favorite band, it is entirely possible to use the name of the band, as long as their music (if rights have not been secured) is never heard. The music leading into the scene need not absolutely correspond to the music Conor is hearing on his headphones. But it then becomes important, if rights have not been secured, that Geoff's singing along not repeat literal lyrics to any song protected by copyright.

GEOFF. I heard that.

KEVIN. Get over here and let's at least pretend to be serious. *(Calling off.)* Guys, get in here! We're starting.

GEOFF. Don't we have to wait for the teacher?

KEVIN. Right. Conor, no shit, your teacher's coming tonight and I think it'd be a wee bit awkward if she comes in and sees you.

> *The two other guests enter from the offstage kitchen, both of them holding wineglasses. Pamela Hosmer is Geoff's wife, dressed as unostentatiously upscale as her husband. Alice Tuan is an International Relations professor at Tufts, a very cool customer. Pamela is already slightly tipsy, effusive in her greeting to Conor. She hugs him.*

PAMELA. Conor!

KEVIN. He's going up to his room. Where he says he'll do his homework but he'll really be watching one of those raunchy internet shows none of us know anything about—

> *[At this point, it's important that the scene allow for carefully choreographed overlapping of dialogue. This is a social gathering, wine has been consumed. They're not going to patiently wait for each other to finish their sentences before saying what they want to say. There are, essentially, two trains of dialogue going on, because Kevin never fully takes his focus off his laptop, and Geoff divides his attention between what's coming up on Kevin's screen and what's going on in the rest of the room.]*

PAMELA. *(The mother who's always got to let the kids know she's hipper than anyone else; her line should overlap with Kevin's last line.)* No, we *do* know about those shows. *High Maintenance*, do you like that one?

CONOR. Sure.

KEVIN. *(Overlapping Pamela, his interest suddenly taken by something on his laptop screen.)* Halcón Resources. Do you believe we're talking about oil again?

GEOFF. *(Referring to what's coming up on Kevin's laptop, which he's leaning over and studying.)* This is stuff we could be getting from *Barron's*.

KEVIN. *(Keying in on what Pamela's just said to Conor.)* Alright, you perfect parents who seem to know every detail of your kids' lives. Tell me, please, how do I get him to get his grades up? Alice, I know how you do it—if Anne-Marie gets anything less than an A you chain her to the castle wall, just out of reach of a glass of water.

ALICE. Just because you can't imagine a more subtle approach, Kevin, don't assume the rest of us need to resort to punitive measures.

> *Behind his father's back, Conor gives Alice a big thumbs up, which Kevin finally notices.*

KEVIN. What, do you two want to bond? Maybe you could matriculate at Tufts and take Alice's International Relations course, Conor.

> *Alice reacts to everything Kevin says about her with a frosty stare. Which is not the same thing as really being offended. A kind of unspoken gamesmanship is going on between these two.*

CONOR. I'd do that.

KEVIN. But first you have to get *into* Tufts, young man. Go study.

PAMELA. Don't let him embarrass you.

CONOR. No, I'm over the embarrassment. G'night.

> *He exits.*

PAMELA. So gorgeous.

KEVIN. Okay, okay. Before she comes. When does the School Committee meet?

GEOFF. Tuesday.

KEVIN. The little study we commissioned—you're going to bring that up.

GEOFF. What little study?

KEVIN. Stop.

GEOFF. You mean the one that shows that Patchett kids are dumber than our kids?

KEVIN. Stop.

GEOFF. No, basically that's what it says. You want me to get up and announce that at the School Committee meeting? Look, folks, look at the gap in SAT scores—150 point average. Why should that matter?

ALICE. Of course it matters. I'd be happy to bring it up.

KEVIN. No, you can't. You're seen as the Antichrist. It's got to be somebody like Pamela. You've got to come up with a soft argument, like, "It'll be too challenging for them."

PAMELA. Except maybe it won't, Kevin.

KEVIN. You want to take that chance? Look, we bring those kids over, we have to take their teachers as well. You want your kids to be taking a class from a history teacher who's been using a textbook printed when there was still a USSR?

ALICE. No.

> *Doorbell rings.*

KEVIN. Okay, that's her. We're going to have to table this, but I'm not letting it go.

GEOFF. *(Taking out his phone.)* Fine. And I'm calling Minimora.

KEVIN. *(Kept from stopping Geoff by the fact that he's on his way to the door.)* No! I spent a fortune on that stuff—

GEOFF. Let's make her feel special, Kevin.

> *As Kevin goes and answers the door to let Cara in, Geoff conducts a conversation with the proprietor of Minimora. We don't have to hear the specifics. He's asking what the specials are, and putting in an order and giving the address. The important thing is that he's on the phone when Cara enters.*

PAMELA. *(To Geoff.)* Make sure you order the miso cod. *(Turning to Alice as Kevin ushers Cara in, so that they're actually in conversation when Cara is about to be introduced.)* Have you had Yuki's miso cod??

ALICE. Of course.

KEVIN. Everybody knows Cara Russo.

> *Cara is taken aback by the fact that these people are familiar to her.*

CARA. Hello. I'm—actually—really embarrassed. I didn't know there would be—parents of my students here.

KEVIN. Oh stop. This is so divorced from school. You know everybody. Alice Tuan, our resident Tiger Mother.

Cara is even more embarrassed by Kevin's remark.

ALICE. He needs to do this. For some reason, he thinks it's funny.

KEVIN. And Pamela Hosmer.

PAMELA. I *loved* your notes on our son's Elie Wiesel paper.

KEVIN. And that's Geoff Hosmer rudely on the phone.

GEOFF. *(Ending his phone conversation with Minimora.)* I'm sorry. It's just for your first time, we thought you should have something better than the processed crabmeat that Kevin considers haute cuisine. I've just ordered eel sashimi.

CARA. I hope Mr. O'Neill explained.

KEVIN. Come on. *Kevin.*

CARA. I'm just here to see if this is right for me.
I hope it doesn't represent a conflict of interest.

KEVIN. Will you stop with the excuses? Have a seat. Have a glass of wine.

> *He pours.*

CARA. No. thank you.

KEVIN. Of course you're going to have a glass of wine. Don't say anything until you've tasted it. And we apologize. We've got to start right off because Alice has a lecture early tomorrow morning.

PAMELA. *(Making a place beside herself for Cara to sit, and inviting her.)* We're really happy you're here. *(As if they're going into a private tête-à-tête.)* Listen, this is going to be over/whelming at first.

KEVIN. Ladies. Ladies \ can we please get started here. Cara is going to be just fine. But the first thing we've got to deal with is the moral issue Pamela brought up last time.

PAMELA. What moral issue?

KEVIN. The Chilean copper mines. Remember? They're restructuring, and if we go in on this we put—how many?—

> *He consults a piece of paper he has handy.*

Three hundred Chileans out of work.

> *At first no one responds. Cara looks ashen. Then Geoff breaks the tension, calling Kevin's bluff.*

GEOFF. What bullshit

Kevin releases a big smile.

We do not invest in Chilean copper mines. This guy is teasing you. I can't believe / you—

KEVIN. I'm \ sorry. I couldn't help it. I wanted to see what you would do. Everybody who comes into this group has to undergo a little hazing.

PAMELA. It's true. You should have seen what he did to me. He pretended we were investing in Chick-/fil-A.

Cara is about to stand, but Kevin gently holds her down, tops off her wine.

CARA. This \ is really not comfortable.

KEVIN. It's a sign of respect. Really. I just want to introduce you to the fact that sometimes, what we do here, sometimes—*sometimes*— is tough stuff.

GEOFF. Oh please. Yet more bullshit. It's Mickey Mouse. "Fun" investments. I personally am always arguing for us to go riskier.

KEVIN. I apologize.

Cara looks at him, expecting more of an apology. Pamela reaches out to reassure her, whispering: "It's just him..."

Okay. Down to it.

GEOFF. I have been reading about event-driven investments.

KEVIN. You're kidding me. / Where have you been reading—

GEOFF. *(Explaining to the others.)* Disney wants to buy some \ upstart animation studio. Let's call it—I don't know—AnimoGraphics.

KEVIN. Brilliant.

GEOFF. And if the deal goes through, AnimoGraphics stock goes way up, and we exploit the pricing inefficiencies.

KEVIN. *Pricing inefficiencies?* Geoff, where are you picking up this / lingo?

GEOFF. I'm look\ing around—I don't know—is it fun just picking conventional stocks? I want to get *in there*.

KEVIN. Excuse me. Alice, Pamela, Cara. Geoff seems to have lifted his investment strategy from that Eddie Murphy movie—

GEOFF. *Trading Places*. I happen to love it, but that's beside the point.

KEVIN. Geoff, in the real world there are men and women who spend eighteen hours a day hunched in lightless cubicles—their entire job is to determine the potential of a deal like Disney buying "AnimoGraphics" actually going through—

GEOFF. So?

KEVIN. So we are a little—social group. We don't have the human resources to—

GEOFF. No, but you do.

> *Beat.*

At Landmark Horizons. At your firm/.

PAMELA. I \ told him he was overstepping.

GEOFF. I mean, you've been a saint, we commend you, but you come to these meetings with information. That we don't have. And sometimes I just wonder how much would it hurt, if just once, you—shared. You shared.

> *Geoff drinks.*

Don't look at me like that. I mean, this has been fun. I just want to have more fun. Alice?

ALICE. I'd love to have more fun. But Kevin can't share that information.

KEVIN. Thank you, Alice.

ALICE. Any more than he can share his countless other dark secrets.

Kevin's talking about the SEC.

GEOFF. I'm just feeling like our strategy's getting a little *sedate*.

KEVIN. *(An edge.)* Sedate? Geoff, you know what you're good at? You're good at organizing bicycle races for cancer research that are really just excuses for aging suburban guys to show off their butts in Lycra shorts. You know what *I'm* / good at?

GEOFF. You know \ how much we raised last year on that ride?

KEVIN. Whatever it was, it wouldn't amount to the monthly return on your trust fund.

PAMELA. I told you you were overstepping.

She looks at Cara: "It's not always like this."

KEVIN. No, maybe Geoff is on to something. Maybe we should institute some secret handshake thing. Or a system of winks. I should mention a company and then wink when I mention it.

GEOFF. That'd work.

KEVIN. Except that, as Alice has told you, if I were to do that I'd likely lose my job and possibly go to jail.

GEOFF. Okay.

There's been some tension.

KEVIN. *(Consulting his laptop.)* This month's recommendation. Is a Canadian oil and gas explorer. Before you shut me up, I know energy is down, and why should it ever come back? And this particular company's shares have fallen forty-three percent in six months.

GEOFF. Sounds like a winner.

KEVIN. But it will be. Trust me. It's going to be back to its high within a year. You want me to explain? The supposed losses have to do with the drop in Canadian currency.

GEOFF. I'm falling asleep.

KEVIN. Take a nap. The rest of you. Alice, Pamela, Cara?

CARA. I'm just listening.

KEVIN. No. That's the one thing that's not allowed. Just to listen. Ask questions. *(To her hesitation.)* The whole thing about money is people are afraid of seeming dumb. Guess what? We're all dumb.

PAMELA. I had to go through this. I'm *still* going through it.

CARA. *(Beat; under pressure.)* All right. Explain the thing about the drop in Canadian currency.

KEVIN. Simple enough. The company reports its operating costs in Canadian dollars, and the loonie's down ten percent. So there's been a panicky sell-off. But they generate revenue in US dollars, so there's actually a favorable foreign currency translation.

CARA. Thank you. You have just made things absolutely clear.

KEVIN. *(Smiles at her.)* We all do our homework here, Ms. Russo. You'll get there. You just need to read the book. *(To the others.)* So.

This company has bought a stake in a natural gas reserve in British Columbia, and it's my recommendation that we go in. It'll take a year, fourteen months.

GEOFF. What else have you got?

KEVIN. There's a company that makes chemical coatings.

GEOFF. Be still my heart.

KEVIN. Niche market. Shares have gained three hundred sixty-nine percent in the last two years.

GEOFF. You have my attention. How have we missed that?

KEVIN. We're getting in late. But maybe not too late. I think it goes up slightly—ten to twenty percent—before it comes down. Alice?

ALICE. If we're careful.

KEVIN. We'll be careful. Pamela?

PAMELA. Yes. Sure. I mean, it's Geoff's money.

GEOFF. *(Touches Pamela's hand.)* It's *our* money.

KEVIN. Cara?

CARA. *(An edge; he's pushing too hard.)* Are you going to give me an explanation as bad as the last one?

KEVIN. I'll try my hardest. Ask.

CARA. *(Accepting the challenge, but clearly annoyed with him for pressing her.)* All right. Why should it keep going up?

KEVIN. Because it's been under the radar. A mystery in and of itself. But if a genius like me has just discovered it, it's going to take another little while before the bozos at Merrill catch on. By which point it will be expensive enough to begin its journey downward. And just before that happens we will, of course, sell. Better?

> *Cara nods.*

All right? We do that one?

> *There's general agreement.*

And how do we feel about our little oil and gas explorer?

GEOFF. Tell me the name. I have an instinct about these things.

KEVIN. You have no fucking instinct at all. Colexico.

GEOFF. I like it.

ALICE. Fourteen months?

KEVIN. That's the outside range.

GEOFF. *(Says this very fast, to match the tempo in which they've been talking.)* Is Landmark Horizons going in?

KEVIN. Not fast enough, Geoff. So. Cara. In or out??

CARA. Don't pressure me please.

KEVIN. This is pressure? On the contrary. This is *fun.*

> *Lights down.*

Scene 4

Cara and Kevin.

The aftermath of the gathering. Empty containers of take out Japanese food. Two bottles have been opened and finished. A nearly empty third one is between them.

KEVIN. So?

CARA. My first question is, why did you embarrass me?

KEVIN. I didn't embarrass you.

CARA. I think it's up to me to say whether or not I was embarrassed.

> *He pours her a glass of wine. She doesn't reject it.*

KEVIN. Refresh my memory.

CARA. The copper mine thing.

KEVIN. Oh. Cara. Do you really want me to treat you with kid gloves?

CARA. It wouldn't be a bad thing. And then the whole way you kept pressing me.

KEVIN. Because I want you in this group. You'd be a breath of fresh air.

Look, if I was too kind, you wouldn't trust me. When you start to play ball with somebody, you throw the ball hard—you don't lob it. You want to test their capacities.

CARA. Thank you. I always enjoy a good sports analogy.

> *She drinks.*

KEVIN. And you have a little drinking problem, don't you?

She puts the wine down, resentful and challenging both.

CARA. Do you work really consciously on being an asshole?

KEVIN. Sorry. I count things. I can't help it, it's a professional failing. How many glasses you've had. It's that it's very good. The wine.

CARA. I don't have a drinking problem. I like to drink. Particularly when I'm feeling a little tense. And this was overwhelming. Moral hazards, securities, derivatives. Can you tell me what a derivative is?

KEVIN. I can, and I will, but look, everything you're hearing is only the poetry of finance. A good guideline is things usually mean the opposite of what they seem to mean.

CARA. I think I'm in over my head.

KEVIN. Fine. The worst thing in the world would be for me to coerce you. Know what I'm going to do? I'm going to put on some Johnny Mathis.*

> *Beat.*

If I were straight, this would be a very different situation, wouldn't it?

CARA. I would say so. But I still think it may be time for me to go. Is Conor—?

KEVIN. Upstairs, but trust me, he might as well be on the moon. He will *never* come down. At this point in the evening he's lost in Slackerland. *(To her hesitation.)* You're not scared of me?

CARA. I'm scared of *this*.

> *He rolls his eyes.*

Okay, let's start with the fact that I live in mild terror of slipping behind, of preventing my daughter from getting the best opportunities because of decisions I made eighteen years ago. Who to marry and get pregnant by, where to live, those decisions that you never believe are going to have such huge repercussions. But maybe I'm *more* afraid of getting into a situation where you can

---

* If you would like to play music in your production, it is the responsibility of licensees to clear any rights to copyrighted music. If rights to a Johnny Mathis song cannot be cleared (the author suggests "It's Not for Me to Say"), other artists that may be substituted are Dean Martin or Blossom Dearie or even Sammy Davis, Jr., per the clearance of those rights with the copyright holder. The point is there should be some irony in Kevin's choice, and the song chosen should be a romantic one.

abuse me because of my ignorance.

KEVIN. Whoa.

CARA. There.

> *She takes another sip of wine.*

KEVIN. So why'd you come?

CARA. I did a calculation. *(To his reaction.)* I knew you'd be impressed by that. Does this man actually want to help me? You'll be happy to know I gave you a sixty–forty advantage.

KEVIN. I think I deserve eighty–twenty.

CARA. Sixty–forty, There is something you want from me, which I will resist giving you.

Sixty–forty. But before I take a step further, tell me how I can trust what little money I have to you—for you to do things I don't fully understand—how do I trust that you are not going to lose it?

KEVIN. *(Beat.)* You know what I would love to do right now? You know what would excite me more than anything has excited me since my first kiss? What I would love would be if you would lay out your financial life for me. Right here. Right now. On paper. Income. Monthly nut. Savings. Potential raises. Mortgage. Equity. Everything. Strip yourself bare.

CARA. Why would that even be interesting?

KEVIN. Because it would be a map of you. An intimate—map—of another human being. A human being I don't get to know in my— daily rounds.

CARA. Now you really are making me nervous.

KEVIN. I'm sorry. I just want to get in there where you live. Because it drives me crazy. There is no *trust*. There are no *guarantees*. There are simply financial instruments that are available to you—that I could introduce you to, that you could easily understand yourself— but you back off, you shy from them because the words scare you. Why should a word like "derivative" scare you? You're far from dumb.

CARA. I am—far from dumb.

KEVIN. So why be dumb about money? Why know everything there is to know about American literature but shy away from knowing the simplest thing about how money works in this country?

CARA. *(Beat.)* Do you have a pen?

KEVIN. I believe I have a pen.

CARA. And paper.

> *Kevin finds paper.*

I make eighty-one thousand dollars a year.

KEVIN. In a rational world, not a bad salary. And take home? Monthly?

CARA. A little bit more than forty-two hundred, I believe.

KEVIN. You believe.

CARA. A little bit more than forty-two hundred.

KEVIN. Okay. We have forty-two hundred. Give or take. And mortgage?

CARA. Fifteen hundred.

KEVIN. High.

CARA. Two mortgages.

KEVIN. Combined, I hope.

CARA. Combined.

KEVIN. Weekly? Groceries. Necessities. Hairdresser?

CARA. I don't always keep track.

KEVIN. Always. Keep. Track.

CARA. Let's say three hundred dollars.

KEVIN. Let's say three fifty. Do you go out?

CARA. Occasionally.

KEVIN. Let's say three fifty. Do you know this is giving me a boner?

CARA. *(Beat.)* I'm going to pretend you didn't say that.

KEVIN. Relax. It's a play-money boner. Nonnegotiable. Insurance?

CARA. House. Car. Two fifty.

KEVIN. One car? You're paying too much. All right, what else? Health insurance?

CARA. Taken out of my salary.

KEVIN. Good. What else? Car payments?

CARA. Two hundred.

KEVIN. Internet. Cable?

CARA. One twenty-five.

KEVIN. Let's add this up. I get thirty-four seventy-five. What else? Electricity. Gas.

CARA. Another two fifty.

KEVIN. Ouch. We've still got four seventy-five a month to play with.

CARA. Things come up. Car repairs. Oil changes. Water bills.

KEVIN. All those pesky little tax bills we get. I'm going to give you— I'm going to say you've got three hundred a month to play with. Please tell me there's no credit card debt.

CARA. There is. And college loans I'm still paying off. That's another four hundred a month.

KEVIN. Eighty-one thousand, and you're in the red. Anything from your ex?

Silence from Cara.

So. Now for the good part. Equity in the house?

CARA. My mortgage is a hundred and fifty thousand dollars.

He doesn't comment, though there is a comment to be made.

The house has been assessed for two hundred twenty-five thousand dollars.

KEVIN. All right, so there's seventy-five thousand dollars. Savings?

CARA. Yes, ten thousand dollars. I inherited a little money from my mother.

KEVIN. So we've got savings and equity of eighty-five thousand dollars.

CARA. I feel a little embarrassed.

KEVIN. Don't. This is nakedness. This is only revealing the embarrassing little mole on the belly, the patch of body hair you never want anyone to see. To the lover, it's all endearing.

CARA. Stop. Stop doing that. Stop the quasi-sexual come-on. Is that how you seduce people in your office?

KEVIN. Okay, apologies. But I get excited at certain prospects. Making the rich more rich, fuck that. But this. *You.* I can change your life.

CARA. By means of oil and gas. What was it, chemical—

KEVIN. —coatings. There are other ways. We can go beyond the bounds of this little club. You can stay in, and learn something while you're here, but we can also do something in addition. A separate account.

> *Beat. She's not letting go of her suspicions, though this is undeniably exciting.*

CARA. Is this all just a challenge to you? Something fun?

KEVIN. It's not unenjoyable.

CARA. Right. And that's exactly what I'm afraid of. You getting your rocks off pulling me into this territory that, even if I were to take baby steps toward understanding, will always terrify me.

KEVIN. And now I'm going to take this away from you.

> *He removes her wineglass.*

Because neither of us should be any drunker as we conduct the next part of the conversation.

CARA. That's offensive.

KEVIN. I want to help you. I sincerely want to help you. But you cannot be terrified.

CARA. *(Beat.)* Our committee is recommending that the two school districts merge. You need to know that I am one hundred percent behind this. I will not be budged.

> *A reaction from him that he tries to hide.*

KEVIN. Fine. If that's what you need to do. It will be defeated when we all vote.

CARA. To be seen.

KEVIN. Yes. Battle stations. Cara. We both know this. Everyone talks about tearing down the wall that separates the haves from the have-nots. And we have to agree—sure, yes, of course we all have to vote the right way. But here, in our private counsels, we know something else. We first need to take care of our own.

CARA. I hate this.

KEVIN. Of course you do. But what we do, Cara Russo, is we vote for all the good things, and at the same time, we load up our boat and head for the deep water. The safe water. We do this for our children. For our children.

> *Beat.*

Are you with me?

> *Beat.*

Are you with me?

> *Beat. She picks up her glass, then puts it down.*

Good. Then let's begin.

> *Lights down.*

Scene 5

> *A hill in Stillwell. Early spring. Six months after the last scene.*
>
> *Conor and Angela are at the front of the stage. Conor has his earbuds in. What we're hearing is what Conor is hearing.*[*]
>
> *The music goes down. A moment of awkwardness. Conor looks at Angela. Takes his earbuds out.*

CONOR. You want to listen?

ANGELA. What is it?

> *Conor holds his earbuds up to Angela's ear.*

No thanks.

> *He puts his earbuds back in.*

CONOR. You mind?

ANGELA. We're supposed to be talking.

> *He takes his earbuds out.*

CONOR. Hmm?

ANGELA. I said we're supposed to be talking.

CONOR. Actually, according to my father, I think I'm supposed to

---

* In the New York production, Animal Collective was again used here. Whatever music is chosen should be in that vein, but the licensee is again responsible for securing the rights to any music not in the public domain.

be seducing you.

She looks at him.

If you were my girlfriend, your mother couldn't very well fail me, could she?

ANGELA. Yes. She could. And she probably would.

I don't think it's about grades. Between the two of them. I think it's about the merger. If he makes her a ton of money, we can move here. And then she won't care so much about making sure it happens.

Conor appears clueless.

The vote on the schools. It's coming up in a week.

Still no response from him.

Do you even care about this?

CONOR. Not really.

He starts to put his earbuds back in. Gets only one in.

ANGELA. Fine then. How do we do it?

CONOR. Do—?

ANGELA. How do you seduce me? Let's just get it over with. Does it happen on this hill—in full view, I mean, of them down / there?

CONOR. I \ was kidding.

ANGELA. Or, like, are you supposed to take me out? Which, I mean, you wouldn't do.

CONOR. Why wouldn't I?

ANGELA. Please.

Beat. She smiles, pleased that she's got his attention.

Do you ever think of what it would really be like—us coming over here? The buses lining up? Us coming off the buses? And the way you'd all look at us? That shirt you're wearing?

CONOR. What about it?

ANGELA. The boys from Patchett could not begin to understand that shirt.

CONOR. It's just a shirt.

ANGELA. It's not just a shirt. It's signage. Tell me something, how do you seduce a girl?

CONOR. What?

ANGELA. Do you want to put your earbuds back in? Would that be easier for you? How do you seduce a girl?

CONOR. You serious?

ANGELA. I've never been seduced. I'd like to know.

> *Conor looks at her, then out in the direction of the audience. He decides to accept her challenge. He smiles.*

CONOR. That's such an old word. "Seduced." I know I'm the one who used it, but—It's like a word from Jane Austen. "He's a 'seducer.'"

> *Again he smiles, this time at her.*

That's not how it happens. Nobody actually "seduces."

ANGELA. Then how does it happen?

CONOR. People just—it happens. You can't construct how it happens. You don't know. You're just together, you're fooling around, and then—.

ANGELA. See, that's what would be weird. We wouldn't know that.

CONOR. What?

ANGELA. Girls—in Patchett—we wouldn't know how to be casual like that. We would want you to seduce us, but we would think we'd need the excuse of being drunk. And you would figure that out. The boys. In ten seconds flat. We would spend all of senior year just trying to figure out how to read you, and that would be our year. And you would know how to read us in ten seconds.

> *Beat.*

Can we stop talking about this?

CONOR. Sure. I mean.

> *He's about to put his earbuds back in, but he stops.*

What do you do over there? You seem pretty smart.

ANGELA. I'm the class poet. That's my identity. I write these poems with like—these big metaphors in them. These seemingly profound metaphors.

CONOR. Cool.

ANGELA. No. Actually. Not cool. Not cool at all. Somebody might be able to tell me why my poems are bad, but nobody's stepped up to the plate yet. None of the teachers at Patchett. To them I'm a genius.

CONOR. So what are you saying?

ANGELA. I'm saying I'm going to go through high school being the genius poet of Patchett High. At graduation they'll let me read the class poem and they'll use words like "amazing" and they'll all say I have a great future ahead of me.

CONOR. I don't know what you're saying.

ANGELA. I'm just mumbling aloud, Conor. I'm just talking as if you still have your earbuds in.

CONOR. They're not in. I'm listening.

ANGELA. *(Beat.)* Okay, then tell me about him. What's he really doing?

CONOR. I think it's safe to assume he's not doing your mother any kind of a real favor. That's not how he works. All I know is he's obsessed with keeping this place—pure.

ANGELA. Is that the word?

CONOR. It's like—here's my dad. When I was like eleven, twelve, he used to drive me out to these big empty high school football fields. These old public school fields, in places like Natick. Waltham. And we'd throw the football around and he'd say, imagine these stands filled, Conor. And I'd be like—this little kid—I'd be like, what are you saying to me? He wants it to be—for me—exactly like it was for him.

ANGELA. He could have sent you to a private school.

CONOR. No. That's the thing. He would never do that. It would spoil something for him. Some idea he has that it's still *public*, so no matter how unfair it is, it's still basically okay.

But—I actually think there's something else. About your mother. You know how sometimes old people, they go to Haiti, they go to Africa, they feel like they need to do something good in the world before they die. Even if it's all just coming out of their boredom, they feel like they need to—. I think—don't get this wrong—I think maybe your mom is my dad's Haiti.

Lights cross-fade to where Kevin and Cara are sitting, lower on the same hill where Angela and Conor have been talking. They've been there for a while, a picnic spread out around them. Maybe we've been aware of them, presences in the dark.

Cara is studying a piece of paper. Kevin leans back.

KEVIN. You're happy with it.

CARA. *(Stunned.)* This is in six months?

KEVIN. This is in six months.

CARA. I wish I understood it.

KEVIN. *(He might be making himself a sandwich as he says this.)* Nobody does. That's your mistake, to think there's some great over-arching order to it. Those guys on Wall Street, you think they understand it? You want to know how bad it was in 2008? Never mind that we were three hours from having ATM machines dry up and refuse to spit out money. Let's say you'd stuffed all your cash into mattresses. We were *four* hours from that money evaporating as well. All money was going to disappear, Cara, and no one, no one could tell you where it went. Here. Have some prosciutto. We're all hanging off a cliff.

CARA. Don't joke with me. Don't tell me about a cliff, please. I hate it when you do that.

KEVIN. All right. Fine.

CARA. I just want to feel—even a minimum of safety. Can you not do that for me?

KEVIN. *(Smiles.)* No.

CARA. *(Playful; something up her sleeve?)* Can I ask you a question?

KEVIN. Of course.

CARA. Knowing you, I feel you should want this merger.

> *Beat. He takes in her question, perhaps with a little disappointment.*

KEVIN. That's the question you want to ask me?

CARA. Is there something else I should want to know, Kevin?

KEVIN. I don't know. Sometimes—you know what I wish?—I wish you'd ask me a different question.

> *Beat.*

Sorry. I'm putting you on the spot.

> *She looks at him. She's been a little unsettled by this last exchange, not certain what he wants from her.*

CARA. Kevin.

KEVIN. *(Beat; taking a moment before backing down.)* No, please, ignore what I just said. Why should I want this merger?

CARA. *(Still unsettled.)* You don't really like Geoff and Pamela. You don't even like Alice Tuan.

KEVIN. I'm very fond of Alice Tuan.

CARA. Look at you. You're a perfect example of exactly who you want to keep out. You've told me you grew up poor, your parents didn't do a damn thing for you, and yet, look how you ascended.

KEVIN. Yes, / but—

CARA. Be\cause you went to a decent public school where you were given a chance. Now we have this opportunity, and you could add your voice to it. You could help make this happen.

KEVIN. You know what you're missing? I wasn't just a kid who benefitted from the old system. I was hungry. Forgive me, I don't drive around the streets of your town and sense *deep* hunger coming from those kids. All I see is hoodies and devices. Hunger is a real thing, Cara, and it's a rare thing. Wherever I was, when I was a kid, I found—powerful men. I rowed out to their yacht.

CARA. Maybe you should be teaching *The Great Gatsby*, Kevin. You want to come into my class as guest lecturer?

KEVIN. Actually, I'd do a very good job teaching *The Great Gatsby*. There are things in that novel I know my way around that—forgive me—you may not know.

CARA. Such as?

KEVIN. Such as, what happened on that yacht? Between Gatsby and Dan Cody. Can you imagine your way into that? What you do with powerful men is, well, you find out what it is they need. Do they need a son, or do they need something else? You do the things you do—those mildly corrupt things you sometimes have to do— so that you can someday have a real son who doesn't have to do those things.

CARA. What was corrupt?

KEVIN. No. I think we save that for when we know each other better. How's he doing, by the way? This boy I'm trying to save

41

from corruption?

CARA. Conor? He's doing better.

KEVIN. But still not great.

CARA. Still not great.

KEVIN. *(Beat.)* Where do you think he could go? I mean, realistically? Where could he get into?

CARA. That's a question for the guidance counselor.

KEVIN. Oh please. Don't throw me to the guidance counselor. That's like me saying, go ask Charles Schwab.

CARA. Okay. What were his first SAT scores?

KEVIN. Not great. I've hired this genius Harvard graduate—this guy who makes violins in Sudbury—he charges three fifty an hour to tutor Conor. His scores will go up. Don't look at me that way. It's a growing industry. Aging slackers from the Ivies who've discovered they can make a fortune tutoring the young slackers of the rich.

CARA. I think you might think about one of those schools—

KEVIN. Oh God, I hate this already. "One of those schools." Go on.

CARA. Grinnell. Or Macalester.

KEVIN. Oh God.

CARA. No. They're good.

KEVIN. But it's not where I *see* him. I went to Boston College. Very decent school. But not—Jesus Christ, you ever *walk* through Harvard Yard? Does that do something to you? Those buildings? And the way those kids look? Those *faces*. Those young faces, and the futures you think of for them, how they can be *safe* in this world. *That's* privilege, Cara. Ever since Conor was a baby, I have thought—get him there—

CARA. *(A little incredulous, maybe even to the point of laughter.)* Harvard?

KEVIN. Sure. Yes. Why not?

CARA. *(Beat.)* Kevin. Conor's not going to get into Harvard. *(To his non-reaction.)* You can't actually be serious about this.

KEVIN. Actually, maybe I am. Why not? His GPA gets up. His test scores go up. He's a gorgeous kid. He's straight.

CARA. Kevin, there are a lot of straight white males going for a limited number of slots at Harvard.

KEVIN. You know, I'm actually jealous of you. You've got a daughter who apparently does all right. Cares about her grades.

CARA. Yes.

KEVIN. You have this edge on me, and you can't even see how you could use it. Talented girl. Poet, right?

CARA. Yes.

KEVIN. How can you stand to hold her back?

CARA. I am not holding her back. I am just not going into this with unrealistic expectations for Angela.

KEVIN. Oh God, you frustrate me. Can we get this fucking vote over with so you can move here and for once have an unrealistic expectation for your kid?

CARA. There's still a chance we can win this fight. And maybe a boy or girl from Patchett gets the shot at Harvard that's been reserved for your privileged son.

KEVIN. And maybe that kid is your daughter. Does that scare you?

CARA. *(The slightest hesitation.)* No.

> *Beat. He's picked up on something in her, the unacknowledged fear.*

KEVIN. Let's get somewhere, Cara. What's it like to sell yourself short, and then force that legacy onto your daughter? Isn't it time for you to do something about that?

> *Then, he sees the children.*

(Calls out.) Conor!

> *Conor and Angela appear.*

You guys been having fun?

CONOR. Sure. This the food?

> *Conor starts to dig in.*

KEVIN. Angela. The class poet. I've heard all about it. Your mother brags.

> *Angela looks embarrassed.*

Conor, you want to go out?

Kevin retrieves a football from among the picnic things.

CONOR. Not really.

KEVIN. Come on. *(A little irritation with Conor.)* You just gonna chow down, Conor?

CONOR. *(A playful defiance.)* Yup. No—going out for the pass.

KEVIN. Your teacher's been suggesting you're an overprivileged boy.

CONOR. Yeah, well, she may be right about that.

KEVIN. Why don't you show her what you're capable of outside the classroom?

No response from Conor, so Kevin turns his attention to Angela.

Angela. You want to go out?

ANGELA. Not unless you really want to embarrass both of us.

KEVIN. Come on. Short pass.

He tosses her a very easy pass. She catches it.

Nice tuck. See? She's capable.

CARA. Kevin, don't. Please.

Conor is not paying any attention at all.

KEVIN. I'd like to see one of your poems sometime.

ANGELA. You're a poetry fan?

KEVIN. I don't think I've read a poem since high school. Yes, I'd like to see.

ANGELA. I don't think so.

KEVIN. Why not?

ANGELA. I think I'd be just as embarrassed as I would be trying to catch an actual pass.

She tosses him back the football. The two of them look at each other a moment.

KEVIN. You know, someday you're going to have this very interesting experience. I'd predict. You're going to be in somebody's office, and they're going to say to you—maybe not in so many words, but still—all right, sell yourself. You're going to have five minutes. And it won't just be what you say. It'll be your eyes, the way you hold your head. Your hands. It'll be about how you seize that moment.

> *Angela looks at him. She's not sure how to take this, but she's intrigued.*

It's never too early to practice. You never know when that moment is going to come. It might be here right now.

CARA. Kevin, she doesn't have to impress you.

ANGELA. *(Soothing her mother, without taking her eyes off Kevin.)* It's okay. This guy is interesting.

KEVIN. *(Beat.)* Conor, do you see how she's handling herself?

CONOR. What?

KEVIN. Get the prosciutto out of your mouth and watch how she's handling herself.

ANGELA. What am I doing?

KEVIN. I don't know, but you're impressing me. I admire a lack of fear.

> *Beat.*

You want to go to Stillwell High, don't you?

> *Beat. She looks at him.*

The eyes say everything. Don't they. Vote's coming up in a week. A great school becomes mediocre or else it stays great, and, if you want, you get to go there. Maybe it's time to remind your mother what's at stake. Remind her what it is to want something.

> *He tosses her the football again. She catches it.*
>
> *Lights down.*

End of Act One

ACT TWO

Scene 1

Kevin's house.

Before the intermission lights in the audience go down— perhaps as they're just starting to go down—Kevin enters and goes to the desk in the corner of his living room. He turns on a jazz ballad, ideally played by a tenor saxophonist.* Then he pours himself a snifter of brandy, sits in the very comfortable reclining armchair adjacent to his desk. He adjusts the light and then the sound, puts on a pair of reading glasses and begins perusing a slip of paper in his hands.

By this time the lights should be fully down on the audience and up on him.

Conor comes on. It's a weeknight. Late. He's wearing a backpack, earbuds dangling around his shoulders. He's wearing a cap on backwards.

CONOR. You're up late.

KEVIN. I am. Interesting reading. Compelling. Your report card.

Conor doesn't respond.

I don't suppose I can ask where you've been.

CONOR. Sure. I'll be honest. You're going to yell at me anyway. At Shana's.

Conor drops his backpack, which makes a noise a little too loud for Kevin, who's fixated on a certain passage in the music.

KEVIN. Shh. You hear that?

Kevin takes a moment to fully appreciate a passage in the music.

---

* The author suggests either Dexter Gordon or Sonny Rollins. It is the responsibility of licensees to clear any rights to copyrighted music. If rights to either of these musicians cannot be cleared, and music from the public domain is used, the music should conform to Kevin's taste.

[In the New York production Dexter Gordon's "Darn That Dream" was used, and the following lines followed "You hear that?" If rights to this specific song have not been secured by the licensee, Kevin's next line should be deleted.]

Dexter Gordon. He's quoting "Polka Dots and Moonbeams." In the middle of one song, he likes to quote another.

CONOR. So let me have it.

KEVIN. What?

CONOR. Pathetic grades.

KEVIN. You characterize them well. End of junior year, too. Not a good time to arrive at a… two-point-three-five GPA. Why are you so fucking lazy?

> *Conor doesn't say anything. He motions for his father to keep it coming.*

Why are you so immune?

CONOR. Not sure.

KEVIN. What would happen if I hit you?

CONOR. Ouch. Not sure about that either.

KEVIN. Knocked you around the room.

CONOR. Ouch.

KEVIN. In thousands of households in America, that's what's happening right now. Report card time. Desperate, disappointed fathers knocking their sons around. For a very good reason.

CONOR. *(Beat.)* We read *Death of a Salesman* in Ms. Russo's class.

KEVIN. *(Appreciating the irony.)* And that told you everything you need to know about desperate, disappointed fathers.

CONOR. I got a B on the paper.

KEVIN. So why's your grade a C?

CONOR. I did fine on *Death of a Salesman*. Slipped up on some of the other stuff she handed us. Edwidge Danticat. Kazuo Ishiguro. Salman Rushdie. Could *not* get through Salman Rushdie. Have we had it?

KEVIN. What?

47

CONOR. The conversation.

KEVIN. I've gotten her a spectacular return in seven months. You'd think she could do me this favor. Why is she making you read this stuff? These books you can't get into.

CONOR. Dunno. Other parents demand it. An "international" curriculum.

KEVIN. She should stick with Willy Loman. This other stuff— who's demanding it? As if I didn't know.

> *Conor just looks at him.*

CONOR. She's a hard teacher. She's—

KEVIN. —incorruptible.

CONOR. Okay.

KEVIN. And you? You don't want to give me this? I worked damn hard to keep your school intact. And guess what? We won. We won the vote.

CONOR. I know.

KEVIN. So you can't even give me this little thing.

CONOR. What little thing? You think I cared about what happened with the school?

KEVIN. What's going to happen to you?

CONOR. Dunno.

KEVIN. *Tell* me. Every other kid—I'm imagining the scene next June, at graduation. Every other kid. Cornell, Colgate, UVA. Alice Tuan's fucking—

CONOR. Anne-Marie.

KEVIN. Exactly. Anne-Marie at MIT. And Geoff and Pamela's fucking—

CONOR. What are you drinking?

KEVIN. I don't know.

> *He lifts the cognac to read the label.*

A gift from a man I made rich.

CONOR. You know Geoff and Pamela's son's name.

KEVIN. Leo. Fucking Leo. God forbid *Leo* should rebel for a second and complicate Geoff and Pamela's perfect life. No. Every other kid doing great. And all the parents congratulating each other. Throwing around the names of schools like—I don't know—like islands in the Caribbean they're about to fly to.

And Conor—beautiful Conor—slipping down the river. What'd I do wrong?

CONOR. Nothing. I mean it. Nothing.

KEVIN. You punishing me for leaving your mother?

CONOR. No.

KEVIN. Okay. That's as deep as I go psychologically. The truth is I don't believe that crap anyway. What I *believe*—is that everybody's got to have a moment. A defining *moment*, Conor, where ambition kicks in. For me—I'll tell you this—it was that book you didn't even bother to read.

CONOR. Salman Rushdie?

KEVIN. Very funny. *The Great Gatsby*, smart guy. My alcoholic Uncle Glenn gave it to me when I was sixteen. You know what it was that got to me? This list Gatsby made as a boy. His father brings it to the funeral. 6:15, rise, 6:45, lift weights, 7:15, study electricity. It was making a plan for yourself and sticking to it that *moved* me. And here's the thing: it's a joke in the book, Fitzgerald wants you to take it as a joke, but you know what? People who want to do well in this country do not laugh at Gatsby's list. It's how we fucking succeed. Getting up and sticking to the list.

CONOR. *(Beat.)* Moving.

KEVIN. Really? That's all you're going to say?

CONOR. I mean it. Moving. I'm going to ignore the slight drunkenness and give you credit for sincerity. It never happened for me.

KEVIN. Yes. Well. Obviously.

CONOR. It seems—fake. I dunno. Running around. Trying to get into a good school. What is that?

KEVIN. Right. So what do you replace it with, Conor? Slacking off? Do you have any idea what rides just beneath our world? The bleakness. Do you have any idea of how most people live?

CONOR. No.

49

KEVIN. So privilege will just guide us through—cushion the blows—you don't have to do anything. Go to a good college? Hell no. *Privilege* will protect you.

CONOR. Look. When I'm ready I'll go to school. Doesn't have to be a great one. I'll do something.

KEVIN. Carpentry.

CONOR. Maybe.

KEVIN. Snowboard instructor in Colorado.

CONOR. Sure. That thing that's important to you—it's a fake thing. To stand with the other parents, in that beautiful green field—you see, I know your mind. I know your fantasies. You all lift the flute of champagne and show your kids off. Conor got into—wherever. Look what a great father I am.

KEVIN. You think that's all it is for me.

CONOR. I *know* that's all it is for you. Your supposed friends. Your little world. Your trophy kids.

KEVIN. You can't believe I want something just for you.

> *Conor is unresponsive.*

> *Beat. Kevin seems overcome by something.*

Come here. *(When Conor doesn't.)* Come here.

CONOR. No. I don't like these little moments where you get so emotional.

> *Kevin goes past this, hugs Conor.*

KEVIN. Just. Let me. Just let me.

CONOR. You finished?

> *Kevin releases him.*

KEVIN. Sure. Go to bed. Sloppy. Sloppy father.

CONOR. It'll be okay.

KEVIN. Never mind that it won't.

> *Conor hesitates a moment, as if to reassure his father. Then he leaves.*

Scene 2

A Starbucks. On the other side of the stage, Angela sits at a counter, a plastic Starbucks cup in front of her, with a straw.
Kevin approaches, having thrown on a sports jacket. He sits beside her.

KEVIN. Sorry I'm late.

ANGELA. It's all right.

KEVIN. I was supposed to buy that for you.

ANGELA. I bought it for myself. It's all right.

KEVIN. It wasn't supposed to be the deal.

Angela sips through the straw.

What is that, anyway?

ANGELA. It's a Frappuccino.

Kevin considers something.

KEVIN. Was it weird, when I called you?

ANGELA. You want me to be honest? Yes.

KEVIN. Okay. These things happen. Maybe I'm feeling a little remorse.

ANGELA. How's that?

KEVIN. I mean—Jesus, I personally financed the whole campaign to keep this merger from happening.

Beat.

Then I read your poems. Your mother showed me. Full disclosure: I asked for them.

Angela sips her Frappuccino.

You're seriously talented.

ANGELA. I have potential.

KEVIN. That's the best you can say about yourself?

ANGELA. That's about the best I'm willing to say.

KEVIN. And what do you want for yourself?
 Tell me.

ANGELA. I'm seventeen years old.

KEVIN. Okay.

ANGELA. I don't have to define things that way.

KEVIN. Do me a favor. Dream a little.

Beat.

Imagine—for a moment—no limitations.

ANGELA. Is that the sort of thing you said to my mother?

KEVIN. The sort of thing, yes.

ANGELA. That she fell for.

KEVIN. Ooh. You're a tough one. My question remains on the table. Don't shy from it. Take a risk.

ANGELA. What I want.

KEVIN. Yes.

ANGELA. It'd be nice to go to a private college.

A little smile from Kevin. Angela picks up on it.

What are you smiling about?

KEVIN. It's 2015. A talented, very smart young girl in the richest country in the world says, "Nice to go to a private college" and it's like saying, "I wonder what the climate of Venus is like."

Beat. Angela sips her Frappuccino.

Let's say you could get into one. Because *of course* you could get into one.

ANGELA. Not one of the really good ones. A decent one.

KEVIN. Grinnell, Macalester.

Angela wonders silently why he's chosen those two.

ANGELA. They wouldn't give me much financial aid. What am I, a white girl? An unspectacular white girl.

KEVIN. Why put yourself down that way?

ANGELA. Why not? Why not see yourself as you are?

KEVIN. *(Smiles.)* When I was your age, I thought I was the bee's knees. *Nothing* was going to stop me.

ANGELA. Good for you.

KEVIN. All right, so let's put you back in your dorm room at Grinnell.

ANGELA. Don't you want a coffee?

KEVIN. I don't drink coffee.

ANGELA. My dorm room at Grinnell.

KEVIN. The money I made for your mother is paying your tuition.

ANGELA. That's—okay maybe that's the problem I have. I don't want her to—if she's made money, if you've made her money—she should have it for herself.

He takes that in.

KEVIN. No kid thinks that way.

ANGELA. She hasn't had it easy. My father skipped out.

KEVIN. Do you see him?

ANGELA. Infrequently.

So she should have it. What's the point of being at just an okay school and her going into debt? I can go to a state school. It's fine. Even that now—they keep raising the tuition. I would carry—

KEVIN. Guilt.

ANGELA. *(Beat.)* Yes.

KEVIN. So what does that leave, a community college?

ANGELA. Most of my friends would be doing that.

KEVIN. Solidarity.

Let me ask you something. Has a great American poet ever come from a community college?

ANGELA. I haven't done the research, but I don't believe Walt Whitman went to Yale.

She sips her Frappuccino.

KEVIN. So clever.

By now she's finished her drink.

ANGELA. What are we doing?

KEVIN. Hmm?

ANGELA. Why'd you want to meet me?

KEVIN. There's got to be somebody who wants me to help them.

She looks at him.

Your mother. One for all and all for one. Stay in that little ghost town over the river. Maybe you can get her to budge.

She still doesn't respond.

ANGELA. What's this about for you?

KEVIN. Look, I know I'm the personification of evil in a lot of ways. I worked very hard to keep a whole—*town* from getting a better chance. And I did that for a very good reason. Because I believe it would, in the end, help no one. What you can do is help individuals.

Beat.

Talented individuals.

Beat.

Tell me the highest dream you have. Don't say "private college." Tell me the highest dream.

Angela is deciding whether or not to trust him.

Come on. Don't hold back on me. This is a Starbucks.

ANGELA. What's that have to do with it?

KEVIN. Come on.

ANGELA. Vassar.

KEVIN. Okay.

ANGELA. I don't know anything about it. A girl—

KEVIN. Yes?

ANGELA. A girl I knew went there. She disappeared from Patchett. I mean, I see her sometimes. Christmas break. She was—really smart. Really pretty. Really—she was cool.

KEVIN. Vassar.

ANGELA. I looked up the tuition.

KEVIN. What? Sixty thousand?

ANGELA. Okay. So now you made me spill this thing. This—dream. Which is not even a dream.

KEVIN. Sure it is. Could you get in?

ANGELA. I don't know.

KEVIN. What do we have to do to get you in?

ANGELA. You're not in charge of my life.

KEVIN. We need to move you to Stillwell. We need to get you into that high school.

She looks at him strangely.

ANGELA. That bus left, I think.

KEVIN. I have made your mother some money. And look, affordability should never be the issue. Trust me, there are ways, if you can get into Vassar, that Vassar will make it possible for you to go there. But first you've got to get in. It's up to you to convince your mother to move here.

ANGELA. That's our choice, I think.

KEVIN. Vassar. See yourself there. Have a fucking dream.

ANGELA. It's not up to you.

KEVIN. Maybe it is. Maybe—credit me at least with this—I have some small insight into what can potentially hold people back. People who consider themselves outsiders.

They look at each other a moment. Is she getting something about him?

ANGELA. What is this, sharing time?

KEVIN. You're as hard as nails, aren't you?

ANGELA. Just don't *equate* us, okay?

She's angry. Kevin holds back from responding right away. Angela gets off her stool, ready to leave.

And at least have the fucking courage of your convictions. If you're saying to us—no help, lift yourselves up by your bootstraps, talent will out—all of that. Have the courage to stick with that.

KEVIN. Where you going?

ANGELA. Home.

KEVIN. Don't. Sit. Please.

ANGELA. You know, maybe if you hadn't spent your money on defeating this thing, if you'd spent your money on trying to help make it happen, we could be having another discussion. You would have helped all of us. And here's the thing—most of us would have failed anyway. Most of us would have chickened out. Not everybody wants opportunity thrown at them. You shocked by that?

KEVIN. No.

ANGELA. But you can't cherry-pick us and have it be okay.

KEVIN. *(Beat.)* You're afraid, aren't you?

ANGELA. No.

KEVIN. You're afraid of Vassar.

ANGELA. No, I'm not.

KEVIN. I'm lookin' at you, Angela Russo. You cannot save your friends. You cannot join the community college crowd and save them all just by being one with them.

I can help your mother move here. We can get you into Stillwell High. And from there, maybe Vassar. Think about it not as some impossible dream you dream in your bed at night but as some real thing. Maybe you don't want to do that, but I am suggesting you could.

> *Beat.*

And one other thing, something you'll hate me for but you already dislike me so why don't I take the next step. That girl who got into Vassar. The cool girl. The really pretty cool girl? I bet she laid off the Frappuccinos.

Small bit of advice, if you want to be serious.

> *Beat.*

Hate me. Go ahead. I'm here to make a dream come true.

Scene 3

> *A booth in an upscale restaurant in Stillwell. Cara and Cathy, both of them drinking margaritas.*

CATHY. *(Perusing the menu.)* Okay. We got charred octopus with Granny Smith, harissa, and endive. Yummy. I don't see nachos here.

> *Cara sips through the end of her straw.*

CARA. Why don't you just go down the menu, and make fun of everything on it.

CATHY. Maybe I'll do that.

CARA. If it makes you feel better.

> Beat. *Cathy sips her own margarita.*

CATHY. Tell me, is there any liquor in this?

CARA. Now you're going to complain about the alcohol.

CATHY. Just saying. Remind me why we're here.

CARA. An experiment. *(Calling off to an offstage waitress, Cara holds up her glass.)* Miss. Another. Please.

CATHY. *(Directing her comments to the offstage waitress.)* Two more. And can you ask the bartender to be a little more generous with the tequila. Like maybe this time actually open the bottle.

CARA. Nice.

CATHY. She deserved it.

CARA. Why don't we just torch this place? It represents everything evil, after all.

CATHY. *(Smiles.)* I like the little mall-ette we're in. Seriously. I like it. Six-dollar cupcakes next door. Why not? Le Cupcake.

CARA. I am seriously hoping there's more liquor in your second drink because I really want to see what you're like when you're uncensored.

CATHY. You moving here?

CARA. *(Beat.)* Maybe.

CATHY. Seriously.

CARA. Seriously. Maybe.

CATHY. This guy's made you a lot of money.

CARA. He's made me some. I could probably rent a place here. And rent my house in Patchett. I haven't decided, but maybe that'd work.

CATHY. So goodbye.

CARA. Please stop.

> Beat. *A more serious moment.*

Why does it matter whether I move or not?

CATHY. I don't know. Let me think on that.

CARA. *(Beat.)* What?

CATHY. I'm seeing it. I'm just seeing it. I'm seeing us meet, where, in a supermarket? No, I don't think so, 'cause you'll start shopping at Whole Foods.

CARA. Cathy, I already shop at Whole Foods.

CATHY. No, but you'll do *all* your shopping at Whole Foods. You'll buy toilet paper at Whole Foods. That's the difference. You'll buy trash bags.

CARA. Mm hmm.

CATHY. So it won't be at Shaw's. Where? Will you still come over and get your car serviced at Ernie's? Maybe there.

CARA. Cathy.

CATHY. What I am seeing is the frailty of the bond. Any bond, Cara. We're not sisters. We don't do Christmas together, or Thanksgiving. What's our big connection? We didn't grow up together. We became friends because we had kids in the same school and we shopped in the same places.

CARA. So I should stay, I should keep my daughter in that pathetic school so that we can meet at Shaw's and share how much our lives suck.

CATHY. Our lives don't suck. I wasn't aware that our lives sucked.

CARA. *(Beat.)* I think we need that drink.

CATHY. No. No. Stop there. Stop sign. How do our lives suck?

CARA. I really don't want to have this conversation.

CATHY. But you opened it up.

CARA. There's a story by Katherine Mansfield.

CATHY. Okay. Go literary on me. Take a big step back.

CARA. Stop it. A story. You read books. A poor little girl in England. Gets invited to a rich girl's house. The rich girl owns a doll house. Inside there's a little lamp.

CATHY. I'm hooked.

CARA. She's not supposed to have been invited. The rich girl's mother throws her out. It doesn't matter. Just getting inside was enough. After she's thrown out, the little girl turns to her sister and says, "I seen the little lamp."

Beat.

We love one another. You and me.

CATHY. Do we? Do we? I mean, I think that's how we like to define it, but how thick is it really? Suddenly our lives, which were perfectly fine—we even had fun—now because you seen the little lamp, everything we had is worthless. It "sucks."

CARA. I believe our friendship is thick, that it can transcend—

CATHY. You moving to this town, and six-dollar cupcakes, and that school, and our kids no longer friends.

CARA. Our kids will stay friends.

CATHY. Right. 'Cause they'll have so much in common. The boys they can talk about.

CARA. Is that all it is, Cathy? They've got to talk about something other than boys. They've got to aim higher.

CATHY. We had our little moments of bliss with boys, Cara. I know your story. I hate when people aren't honest. We both had that, okay? Then they left us and we bring up their kids. That is the story of the world, Cara.

CARA. It doesn't have to be.

CATHY. No?

CARA. Because nobody told us to care about ourselves first. Nobody told us that. And say what you will about that man, that is what he is saying to me.

CATHY. Care about yourself.

CARA. Yes. And it is the hardest goddamn thing anybody's ever said to me.

Beat.

CATHY. Okay. Are you going to cry?

CARA. No.

CATHY. Go ahead if you want to. Don't be embarrassed.

CARA. I want you to support me in this. I am doing this for Angela.

CATHY. You saw your opening, you took it.

CARA. You can be so harsh.

59

CATHY. Tell me this—do you think Angela's smarter than Britney?

CARA. *(Beat.)* Cathy.

CATHY. Tell me.

CARA. I don't know.

CATHY. You have an opinion. Be honest.

CARA. It's not the point.

CATHY. Deflect, deflect, deflect.

> *Beat.*

I'll tell you what I think. No. No, Angela is not smarter than Britney. Ooh, the way it comes down to this. Two mothers catfighting in an upscale dive. But let's be those two catfighting mothers, shall we? Your kid is not smarter than my kid. The difference is a man came along and bribed you.

CARA. He did not bribe me.

CATHY. And bribed you. And now they have—our two sweet little girls—they now have two very different potential futures.

CARA. He did not bribe me. Tell me, what did he get for his bribe?

CATHY. I don't know. You tell me.

> *Beat.*

And it sucks. But there it is.

CARA. And this is the way it works, isn't it? God forbid one of us should get ahead.

CATHY. You got lucky.

CARA. I did. And maybe I'm going to seize this moment of—luck.

> *Alice Tuan enters, on her way to a table. Cara considers whether to stop her. At the last minute:*

Alice!

> *Alice stops, recognizes Cara. She's friendly enough, but Alice is never going to express great warmth.*

ALICE. Hello. Cara. I've never seen you here.

CARA. First time.

ALICE. Well. Another meeting Thursday.

CARA. Yes.

ALICE. See you then.

 Alice exits. A brief silence at Cara and Cathy's table.

CATHY. She your friend now?

 Beat.

Thanks for introducing me.

Scene 4

 Cara's house. Angela enters, coming home from her shift at a fast-food restaurant. She's wearing a uniform.

 Cara is a couple of beats behind her, having driven her home. [This scene is meant to take place just after the last scene, so Cara is wearing the same clothes.] She drops her keys on a table.

CARA. You going to bed?

ANGELA. Think so.

CARA. How's the summer reading going?

ANGELA. *(Shoots her mother a look.)* Please do not bug me about the summer reading list, okay?

CARA. Just wondering what radical choices Patchett High has made this year. What's on it—*Old Yeller? Two Years Before the Mast?*

 They're close enough now that Angela can smell something.

ANGELA. God, I don't know which of us smells worse. Me of French-fry grease or you of—what is this?

CARA. Margaritas. I had a very difficult night with Cathy. The battle of the margaritas. We were both too upset to eat. I must have spilled some.

 She tries to blot a stain out.

ANGELA. Where'd you go?

CARA. That place. L'Espace. In Stillwell.

ANGELA. Ah.

CARA. Everything now is "ah." Everything now is battle lines. I eat in Stillwell and it's like I'm entertaining Nazis in occupied Paris.

ANGELA. Nobody said anything.

CARA. Exactly. "Ah."

ANGELA. *(Beat.)* How is it, L'Espace?

CARA. The second and third margaritas were very good.

ANGELA. *(Amused.)* And you drove me home on three margaritas and no food? No wonder you were so silent.

CARA. But now we need to talk.

ANGELA. I know we do, but maybe not *right* now.

CARA. No. It's July. If you're going to Stillwell High in the fall you need to be reading the books on their summer reading list.

ANGELA. *(Beat; a little taken aback.)* So when are we moving?

CARA. I'm going to start to look at places.

ANGELA. To rent.

CARA. Mm hmm.

ANGELA. I thought you felt differently.

CARA. Maybe I did. Maybe I felt it was only worth something if all of us could rise. Maybe I feel differently now. Frankly, I am a little sick of the mindset that says we have to be loyal to something that no longer works.

ANGELA. *(Starting to go.)* I need a shower. I don't like the smell of the grease.

CARA. Maybe that's exactly the smell that should accompany us during this conversation.

ANGELA. *(Beat.)* What if I don't want to? Go to Stillwell High.

CARA. What's your argument?

ANGELA. For—?

CARA. Staying.

ANGELA. Dunno. Maybe I don't want him to win.

CARA. How does he win? If we go there, if you get to have a future, how exactly is that him winning?

ANGELA. Dunno.

CARA. Don't give me "dunno." "Dunno" is for girls who don't go to college.

ANGELA. You know what it's like, looking at you now? Listening to you? *Invasion of the Body Snatchers*.

CARA. Really? That doesn't seem extreme to you?

ANGELA. We lost. The vote. We lost. If we'd all been able to go there—

CARA. Oh please.

ANGELA. That was your position, what, two months ago?

CARA. Yes, and then we lost. And I had to take in what losing meant. I want you to look at some places with me.

ANGELA. I like this house.

CARA. This house—sucks, Angela. I wish there were a better word, but there isn't. There are spores in the basement.

ANGELA. We hardly go in the basement.

CARA. Yes, but they get sucked up through the heating vents and years from now we're sick.

ANGELA. What are you talking about?

CARA. We allow ourselves to be victims because we think we're too poor, or unlucky, to change our situations—

ANGELA. You know what you sound like? Like somebody who's just read a sociology book and allows it to change the whole way they see the world. Suddenly it's all "victimization."

CARA. *(Cutting through.)* You have one year left, Angela. And I know you're scared.

ANGELA. *(Beat.)* I don't know who I'm talking to.

CARA. I know you're scared. Because for years—maybe I've done this to you—it's been enough for the two of us to be smarter than everybody around us. Me being friends with Cathy. Pretending I don't feel superior, when I do.

> *Beat. Angela just looks at her.*

You and Britney.

ANGELA. So?

CARA. You're smarter than Britney.

ANGELA. I—that's debatable.

CARA. You're smarter than Britney. You deserve a better chance.

ANGELA. Mom.

CARA. Never mind the pathetic debate team at Patchett High. Let's admit the truth here, okay? Britney will be pregnant inside of a year. Like her mother was.

ANGELA. Jesus.

>*Beat.*

I wish you hadn't had three margaritas.

CARA. But I did.

And now I need to tell you, I have made this decision. We are going to rent a house in Stillwell. An apartment, anything. You will go to Stillwell High. We will drive together. It will be nice. I'll get you the summer reading list and you will begin reading those books and you will be in—Mr. Shachter's class—and you will get into a school you *want*—and I will afford it.

>*Beat.*

And I will feel good about myself for the first time in my life.

ANGELA. Wonderful for you. And meanwhile I won't know a soul.

CARA. That won't matter.

ANGELA. Won't it?

CARA. What is that phrase? "Eyes on the prize."

ANGELA. What prize? I will not know a soul. I am not a cool, pretty girl who fits in. I will walk through the corridors hoping somebody says hi to me.

CARA. It won't matter. Your poems will get a serious look. You will be known for your poems.

ANGELA. What if I don't write poems? What if I stop writing poems?

CARA. Why would you do that?

ANGELA. Because they come out of *this*. This life. The two of us here. That school. This house with the spores coming up. This stupid job. If they're good, they're good, if they're bad, they're bad, but they are real.

CARA. Don't—I'm just hearing fear now.

ANGELA. Yeah, maybe you're right, maybe I'll write the best poem

I've ever written about the two of us in that car—taking that drive—from our apartment in Stillwell to the school where my glorious future is supposed to happen. Two women completely alone. "Eyes on the prize." Waiting for a stupid envelope. Congratulations, you got into—blank. Fill in the blank.

CARA. Vassar.

ANGELA. *(Beat.)* How'd you know that? He told you?

CARA. Vassar. And then you're there. And everything changes.

ANGELA. Does it? Does it? I liked what we had here.

CARA. You always said you weren't getting enough.

ANGELA. Okay. Okay, let's say this—we stay here, I do super well this year, I get into the best college I can possibly get into, whatever college gives me enough money. It's not going to be Vassar but so what? We make it work financially in a way that doesn't cripple you.

CARA. Why should that be enough?

ANGELA. Because it allows us to be free of him. Take your money now, cash out—whatever you've got—we'll make it be enough.

CARA. I don't think it's enough.

ANGELA. Suddenly it's not enough. More than we've ever had—

CARA. I need him to make me more just to make your plan work.

ANGELA. I could take a year off after school.

CARA. And work in food service? Come home smelling—

ANGELA. Why not?

CARA. Because why should it be? Why should you have to do that when there's money to be made just by touching his world—just by rubbing up against it? That world exists, Angela. I got lucky.

ANGELA. I don't think so.

CARA. Right, because we need to be pure. We need to believe that world is not for us. Push it away. Money? No, no thanks. Somebody else. Who? If not us, who?

ANGELA. I'm going to bed.

CARA. Tell me. Be honest. Be absolutely honest. That you wouldn't like to put your work in front of a teacher—of teachers—who are ready to take you seriously. And criticize you. And steer you toward

65

a place that will challenge you. Tell me you don't want that and we can end this discussion and stay here and live happily ever after.

ANGELA. Stop.

CARA. And I will go on eating nachos with Cathy on Friday nights and drinking too much.

ANGELA. Stop.

CARA. Tell me. Go ahead. Say it. You don't want that. You want mediocrity. You're happy with mediocrity. You're happy with this.

ANGELA. *(Crying.)* Stop.

> *Beat.*

Can I go to bed now? I don't want to talk about this.

CARA. *(Beat.)* Yes. You can go to bed.

> *Angela goes off. Cara is alone a moment, but Angela comes back, carrying a small stack of paperback books.*

ANGELA. These are the summer reading.

> *Cara takes one of the books.*

CARA. Oh God. I loved this. *Our Town.*

> *She takes another. The cover is very frayed.*

God. *Brave New World.* Are they still teaching this?

ANGELA. *(Interrupting her.)* You're right.
You're right I'm scared. But maybe I want it.

> *She's not looking at Cara as she speaks.*

CARA. Angela, look at me and say that.

ANGELA. Don't. Don't make me say it again. I said it.

CARA. *(Looking at her a long moment.)* Okay.

ANGELA. *(Deep fear, resolve.)* Okay.

Scene 5

Kevin's house. Kevin at his desk at home. Evening. Another jazz ballad by a tenor saxophonist. He's wearing glasses, drinking cognac, studying something on his open laptop.*

Cara enters, holding a small packet of papers. She looks bereft.

CARA. *(Referring to the packet in her hand.)* What's this?

KEVIN. *(Startled.)* Woo. You scared me. What? Let me see. How'd you—?

CARA. Your door was open. I rang. You didn't hear.

KEVIN. Sorry. Let me—

> *He turns down the music, takes the packet from her hands, reads.*

It's your monthly statement.

> *Cara shakes her head.*

CARA. Kevin, I've lost—

KEVIN. What?

CARA. A *third*—

KEVIN. *(Looks more carefully.)* This month. Okay. There's been a correction—everybody's felt it. I had a feeling I'd be hearing from you.

> *Kevin begins tapping into his laptop to draw up her account.*

CARA. Well, you're *hearing* from me. Kevin, I am looking at places in Stillwell.

I need to establish residency next month if Angela's going to go to school here. I need to draw on this if I'm going to make it work. You told me to do this.

KEVIN. China's been a problem.

CARA. If I rent a new place, if I don't manage to rent my own house right a/way—

---

* In New York, Dexter Gordon's "I Guess I'll Hang My Tears Out to Dry" was used. Whatever song or artist is chosen, the licensee is again responsible for securing rights to music not in the public domain. And whatever artist is chosen, ideally it should be the same one Kevin referred to in Act Two, Scene 1.

KEVIN. The \ currency devaluation has been a bitch.

CARA. What?

KEVIN. You read the paper, Cara? You read the business section? You read *Barron's*? You read the *Wall Street Journal*? Do the words Shanghai Composite Index mean anything to you? Because they should. That is, if you're looking for an explanation of this.

CARA. Kevin, we have to have a talk about this.

KEVIN. Clearly. Yes we do. But not if you're going to freak out about it.

Look. I told you. I spelled it out. It goes up, and it goes down. I wish there were a more sophisticated way to explain it. There is not.

CARA. I can't commit to a place in Stillwell if this keeps going down. I did the math. With what I'm going to be spending just to live here, if this doesn't go up, everything I have could be wiped out in a year. I can't do this without confidence.

KEVIN. Cara, Cara, Cara. What have I been telling you since Day One? You cannot have absolute confidence. You have to take a chance. Be bold, young woman.

He hands her back her statement.

CARA. What are you suggesting I do?

KEVIN. Do you like Dexter Gordon?*

CARA. What?

KEVIN. I like Dexter Gordon.*

He sits back, listens.

CARA. Was this your plan all along?

KEVIN. Was what my plan?

CARA. To debase me this way. To take me to a place where I was ready to say, yes, okay, I see it now, I see it your way, I give up, I give in, and then snatch it away from me?

He just looks at her.

Was that your plan? To punish me for giving your son low grades.

---

* If rights to use a Dexter Gordon song cannot be cleared, and another musician's work has been substituted—one for whom rights have been cleared by the licensee—then the name can be substituted, as in, "Do you like Sonny Rollins? I like Sonny Rollins." If using music in the public domain, that name can be used as well, as long as the musician in question conforms to Kevin's taste. (See Notes on Music at the back of this volume.)

KEVIN. Cara.

CARA. It feels like it was.

KEVIN. You're panicking. Panic is bad. Panic is our enemy.

CARA. Can you promise me it will go up again?

KEVIN. No I cannot.

> *Beat.*

I cannot absolutely promise.

CARA. Then I want it out. Now. Before it's all gone.

KEVIN. Fine. You can cash out. Give up every dream. Do not move to Stillwell. Consign Angela to Wachusett Community College. They have an excellent program in physical therapy, I understand. Nothing wrong with that. Lots of girls do it.

CARA. What's my choice?

KEVIN. Risk. Courage.

> *She starts to shake her head.*

This is a piece of *paper*, Cara. This is *nothing*. We all skate on thin ice. The ability to live in the world of money is not to look down, that's all. All of us, we don't look at our monthly statement and say, "Oh my god that's all I've got?" We *assume*. We *imagine*. We *float*. Can you really not do this?

CARA. No. I can't. I can't *float*. Whatever language you want to use, I'm from another world, and I need to know certain things. I'm not trained to think like you.

KEVIN. Then train yourself. If you want your kid to have certain opportunities, you need to train yourself to think differently. Think like a fucking *winner*, Cara.

> *She bridles at this. He takes a long moment before offering the next thing.*

Or—

CARA. *(Looks hopeful.)* Or?

KEVIN. There is another option. One I guarantee you won't like.

CARA. *(Beat.)* Tell me.

KEVIN. I can put your money somewhere else.

CARA. Where?

KEVIN. I can't tell you that.

CARA. Something illegal?

KEVIN. *(Smiles.)* I don't really like that word.

CARA. Then what?

KEVIN. There are synonyms I prefer.

> *Beat.*

Questionable. Morally questionable. Let's go with that one.

CARA. Tell me.

KEVIN. *(Rubs his eyes.)* Do you remember—the first time you came to a meeting at this house. Geoff suggested something.

CARA. No.

KEVIN. He suggested I use what I know—what I do—the investments I make at my firm—the knowledge I pick up at Landmark Horizons—to make us all money.

CARA. I don't remember.

KEVIN. Because you weren't paying attention. I shut him down. But—let me be quite honest with you. I do not lose money at Landmark Horizons. I beat the market or else I go out of business. I could find a way—it's morally questionable, mind you—to help you, based on information I am legally forbidden to use.

CARA. No.

KEVIN. Okay. Done. We'll go back to the wild, uncertain world of the stock market. I'll move some of this around. Of course this will reflect some losses for a while.

CARA. How long?

KEVIN. Probably months.

CARA. I don't have that kind of time. It's going to be Angela's senior year.

KEVIN. Cara, I am deeply sorry that the glorious above-board American system has not timed out so that you can feel secure and cozy with your investment strategy and drive off into the beautiful sunset of all those TD Ameritrade commercials with white-haired couples throwing sticks to their dogs.

CARA. Stop it please.

KEVIN. Given that, we are left with choices. You could accept a loan from me. The Kevin O'Neill Scholarship—

CARA. I've told you I won't do that. I am a teacher in this town.

KEVIN. —or we go to the next level.

CARA. I will not do something—

KEVIN. Corrupt.

He sips cognac.

Sure you don't want some?

When I was a young man. Just starting out. A Boston College grad in a world of Harvard and Yale boys. Smart, slick Cambridge and New Haven lads. Throwing around references I could barely comprehend. Straight boys. Deeply straight boys. And me, pretending—brilliantly—to be one of them. A man asked if he could fuck me.

Beat. She says nothing. He pours her cognac. She accepts it.

This was a married man, mind you. A man I was more or less repulsed by, but one who was in a position to help me. A man who perhaps saw some part of me I had not sufficiently hidden. So what did I do? Take a guess.

She doesn't answer.

Of course I did. But he kept the deal. He delivered on his promise and got me a better job.

Now I look back, I'm not ashamed at all. What I'm struck by now is the simple honesty of that exchange. Giving myself to someone I considered a little repulsive, but understanding, in that transaction, that I was only being honest in a way I'd maybe never fully been before. Naked and basically defiled in a hotel room on Arlington Street, I felt weirdly, powerfully alive.

Now it's your turn.

CARA. Won't you be in danger?

KEVIN. Yes.

CARA. So why?

KEVIN. Because I don't mind danger. What have I really got to lose? This house?

He makes a face: The house doesn't mean that much.
I'd almost like to lose everything just to teach Conor a lesson.

Beat.

So what are we going to do?

CARA. *(Beat.)* How would it work?

KEVIN. *(Takes in her seeming agreement.)* You would never know anything. You would close your eyes and wake up and there would be a better outcome. Like waking up from a medical procedure.

CARA. No. No. No. I am not going with you.

KEVIN. *(Beat.)* Fine. Maybe the market will tick up. Maybe it will all go well for us.

CARA. It's not China, is it?

KEVIN. What?

CARA. You put me in things that you knew would tank so that you could have me in this position. To prove I'm corruptible. Like you.

KEVIN. Don't you teach English? Is that how novels work?

She gets up, as if she's about to go.

CARA. No. I was a fool. A man does not come—into a woman's life—and hold out a promise like this and fulfill it. I was a fool to believe that.

KEVIN. Did you believe it?

CARA. Yes. I did. You were saying the right things to me. Don't live in the small, tight, limited world. Break out. But once you break out, where are you? Where are the boundaries?

KEVIN. Okay, stop. Here's what you're not getting—in your little, psychologically pathetic reading of this situation—the risk would be all mine. We're found out, *I* go to jail.

Beat.

And the motivations—they would have a field day. He secretly loved her. He wasn't really gay, and all this was a way of getting her into bed. What nobody would ever assume is that maybe I am just a decent man. Trying to do a good thing.

CARA. Goodness? Is that what you tell yourself? Breaking the law, Kevin?

KEVIN. Breaking the *law*? Did you really just say that? I am fighting for *you*. My incorruptible friend. Jesus Christ, why not let another side of yourself out? Maybe there's something to be discovered in not being so beholden to virtue. Let *me* be the good one. *You* be fucking ruthless. *You* be Kevin O'Neill. You be the one to stand up naked in a hotel room and say, this isn't so fucking bad. *This* feels like *power*.

She seems to be listening. He leans forward.

CARA. *(Beat.)* So I do this. I allow you to do this. And where does that leave me? My daughter goes to Vassar. Maybe I show up on campus with Angela. She knows. I know. We've both gamed the system.

KEVIN. Unlike ninety-nine percent of the parents you will meet that happy day on the Vassar campus. All of whom have gamed the system in their own way. Genetics. Inheritance. Good zip codes. The ability to pay to artificially induce higher SAT scores. Oh, you are so right. It would be a terrible, terrible thing to game the system. *Nobody* does it.

She looks at him.

Don't you want to face up to all those privileged people on the Vassar campus and say, "Fuck you, I'm here too. *My* kid." Wouldn't that be something? All those Chinese paying full freight, endowing a building just so that their kid can get in, and you saying, *My kid*. All those trust funders who have never had to worry for a second about their kids' futures. And *you* there. You and your daughter. Saying *fuck you. We're here, too.*

CARA. Is this your goodness speaking, Kevin?

Beat.

Take my money out. Please.

KEVIN. Are you thinking of your daughter? Are you allowing fear to rule you, Cara? Fear and smallness and—fear.

CARA. Take my money out.

KEVIN. Ten seconds. Shall we give it ten seconds.

She smiles, very faintly. Then she leaves. Kevin, alone.

We'll call that ten seconds.

He takes a final sip of his drink.

Scene 6

Graduation. A year later. The high school principal (offstage) introduces Angela.

VOICE OF PRINCIPAL. And now it's my great pleasure to introduce our 2016 Class Poet. Angela Russo.

> *Applause, and Angela takes the podium. Graduation cap and gown.*

ANGELA. My poem is called "Trees."

> *She reads.*

Does one tree know what the other tree did to get there?
The troubles of the tree.
To break the earth and plant its web of life in the crowded soil
The painstaking time spent growing and converting sunlight
    into energy?
Does the native tree know the foreign trees' struggles?
—Of course—
It, too, was a foreigner one time

I read in a magazine that if one tree struggles in the forest
The grandmother tree sends it nutrients.
For it wants to see the little tree thrive
Even if the little tree is too small to pierce the canopy to reach
    the sunlight
It happens all the time.

We find it amazing that one tree will help another
But is it such a feat?
Many do the same
A mother changes her life to help a struggling child
An alpha wolf lies next to the runt of the litter
Why are these not reveled in?

Does it have to be death defeating to awe us?
A mother making a deal with a strange man behind the sex

club to get her child into a better school?
Is that risqué enough for us?
Are we numbed to the small feats that occur all the time
—A tree helping another tree grow—
How is that different than the mother or the wolf?

Thank you.

> *Applause, and as it dies down, and the lights go down on Angela, Kevin enters with champagne in a bucket. He places it on the ground. He's on the grounds of the high-school football field, where graduation has been held. He looks around, expectant.*
>
> *Cara enters. She's dressed for a celebration. Beat.*

KEVIN. Hi.

CARA. Hi.

KEVIN. I liked her poem. It was good.

CARA. According to her, it could have been better.

KEVIN. A little close to the bone. We never met behind a sex club.

CARA. No.

KEVIN. Still—some promise. Maybe she'll get there.

CARA. Yes.

KEVIN. Class Poet of Patchett High. Shall we—?

> *He's referring to the champagne. She assents.*

CARA. *(While he pops the cork.)* You know, you were never really good for my sobriety.

KEVIN. No. I know. I'm the devil. And I'm drinking more myself. Putting on weight.

> *He pours.*

There. To their futures. Angela and Conor.

> *They drink.*

You know, it's not so bad here.

> *He's looking around the grounds.*

I mean, I expected—what? More decline? They keep it up nicely.

CARA. It's where the money goes in schools like this. The football team. The grounds.

There's this tacit understanding, I think, that this is going to be the best part of their lives. So make it, at least, nice.

KEVIN. Conor got into Oberlin, by the way.

CARA. Yes, I heard.

KEVIN. I mean, it's not Harvard, but it's something. Sometimes kids turn a corner senior year.

CARA. Yes, sometimes they do. I read his essay.

KEVIN. For the Common App. It was good, wasn't it?

CARA. Sometimes kids turn a corner senior year and start writing like J.D. Salinger.

KEVIN. *(Beat.)* Are you accusing me of something, Ms. Russo?

CARA. Never.

KEVIN. It was his SATs really. They went up. That guy I hired.

CARA. The violin maker. In Sudbury.

KEVIN. Yes.

> *Beat.*

Angela's going to—?

CARA. Wachusett. Two years. Your nightmare for her. Two years, and then we'll try for the private college of her dreams. Her choice.

KEVIN. I'm sorry—the market.

CARA. Don't. I've reinvested, with someone else. The returns are modest, but at least they're going up. So maybe in two years. If the market keeps going up.

> *Kevin nods.*

KEVIN. And maybe it will.

CARA. Why did you come?

KEVIN. I like these things. I'm moved by these things. This last part of what's—American. The old dream. Equal playing fields.

Somebody told me—you're going to love this story—at a private school one of my investors' sons goes to—they need to build a landing pad. The son of a sheik from the Arab Emirates goes there, and the sheik will be landing for his son's graduation by helicopter.

76

CARA. What a world.

KEVIN. Yes. Shall we finish this?

CARA. No.

> *She puts her glass down.*

No.

I've been thinking about the last thing you said. About goodness. About goodness making you want to risk—

KEVIN. Myself?

We've never managed to tell each other everything, have we, Cara?

CARA. No. We haven't.

KEVIN. *(Putting down his glass, as though about to make one more approach.)* So.

> *Beat. She regards the glass he's just placed on the ground.*

CARA. Angela's waiting for me.

KEVIN. *(Beat; taking in the final rejection.)* Yes. Well. Good luck.

CARA. Yes.

KEVIN. Goodbye, Cara Russo.

> *He picks up the champagne bottle and bucket, looks at her, then goes off.*
>
> *Cara watches him. Then she waits.*
>
> *Cara has a moment alone, before Angela appears, in her graduation robe.*

CARA. Ready?

ANGELA. *(Beat.)* Ready.

> *Lights down.*

End of Play

PROPERTY LIST
(Use this space to create props lists for your production)

SOUND EFFECTS
(Use this space to create sound effects lists for your production)

NOTES ON MUSIC

Kevin's musical tastes veer from irony in pop music to a deeply informed appreciation of jazz, particularly of tenor saxophonists of the postwar era, and any choices as to what music is used in the play should conform to these tastes. The author has suggested in Act One that Kevin play a Johnny Mathis tune, ideally "It's Not for Me to Say," but if rights to that song are not available, a song in similar vein can be played, so long as it remains an ironic choice. Acceptable substitutes might be Dean Martin's "Return to Me," or Blossom Dearie's "Mad About the Boy," or even Sammy Davis, Jr.'s "What Kind of Fool Am I?"

Kevin unapologetically appreciates these kinds of songs for their romantic kitsch. But when it comes to jazz, there should be no kitsch. The author has suggested Dexter Gordon, but Sonny Rollins would be a perfectly acceptable substitute. If music in the public domain needs to be used, it should be one of the classic artists of the prewar period, but as very few of these recordings are in the public domain, careful attention needs to be paid.